AI Unleashed: Hack Your Creative Brain Without Code

A Beginner's Guide to Using AI for Writing, Art, and Creative Projects

Author: Nicholas Heruska

This book is a work of nonfiction. Some names and identifying details may have been changed to protect the privacy of individuals. While every effort has been made to ensure accuracy and functionality of the information and tools referenced herein, the author and publisher make no representations or warranties regarding the outcome of using any of the resources, tools, or methods discussed. Use them at your own discretion.

Chapter 1: The AI Creative Party **3**

- My First Time with AI (Spoiler: I Was Hooked)

- No Tech Degree? No Problem

- What You'll Find in These Pages

- Who This Book Is Actually For

- One Quick Win to Get You Hyped

Chapter 2: Flipping the Creative Switch with AI **17**

- My Lightbulb Moment That Changed Everything

- Why Your Brain Loves a Bot

- Creativity vs. Overthinking (And How AI Helps)

- Weird but True: Science Behind AI Imagination

- Quick Wins to Try Right Now

Chapter 3: My Favorite Free AI Tools **35**

- The Treasure Chest You Didn't Know Existed

- AI Tools That Feel Like Magic

- Free Beats Paid (Most of the Time)

- Setup So Simple It's Silly

- What Each Tool Does Best

- Playground Tour: Try This One First

Chapter 4: Writing with AI... **52**

- Beating Writer's Block with a Robot Sidekick

- Prompts That Hit Hard

- Editing So It Still Feels Like *You*

- Spicing Up Boring Paragraphs

- How I Wrote a Story in 6 Minutes

- Remixing Classic Plots with AI

- Try This: Write Something Weird

Chapter 5: Making Art with AI **69**

- My "Bad Art" Origin Story

- Free AI Art Tools I Swear By

- Turning Ideas into Gallery-Worthy Pieces

- The Wild World of AI Style Prompts

- Fan Art, Portraits, and Meme Chaos

- From "Meh" to "Whoa": Editing with AI

- Make This: Your First AI Art Challenge

Chapter 6: AI Music from My Bedroom...................... **85**

- How I Accidentally Produced a Lo-Fi Hit

- Sound Tools That Feel Like Toys

- Beats on a Budget

- Jamming Solo or with AI Collaborators

- Writing Lyrics with Bots

- Mixing Tricks Even DJs Will Respect

Chapter 7: Brainstorming Like a Maniac 100

- Generating a Hundred Ideas in Ten Minutes

- Prompts That Blow Minds

- What Makes an Idea Stick

- Creative Filtering (aka Choosing the Gold)

- AI as a Thought Partner, Not a Boss

- My Favorite "WTF" Ideas

Chapter 8: Side Hustles Supercharged by AI 117

- How I Turned a Random Prompt into a Paycheck

- AI-Powered Etsy Ideas

- Ghostwriting with Bots (Ethics Chat Included)

- Selling AI Art Without Selling Your Soul

- Micro-Hustles You Can Start Today

- Try This: Product Prompt Game

Chapter 9: AI for Personal Growth 131

- Boosting Confidence Through Creation

- Journaling with AI (Yes, Really)

- Dreaming Bigger with Digital Help

- Reflection Prompts That Don't Feel Cheesy

- When I Realized I Was Playing Small

Chapter 10: Me + AI = Creative Chemistry 143

- How I Stay in Control of My Voice

- Using AI Without Sounding Like It

- Collaging Old-School + New-School Creativity

- When to Go Full Analog

- Making It Feel Like *You* (Always)

Chapter 11: Taming the AI Overwhelm 155

- When It's All Too Much

- FOMO, Burnout, and Decision Fatigue

- My "Unfollow the Robots" Ritual

- Boundaries That Keep Me Sane

- A 3-Step Reset When You're Drowning in Tools

Chapter 12: My Ultimate AI Writing Playbook 168

- ChatGPT Confessions

- Prompts That Unlock Gold

- Editing Like a Real Writer

- Getting Weird with It

- Fanfiction, Essays, Bios—All in the Mix

- What Not to Do with AI Writing

- A Daily Writing Routine You Can Steal

Chapter 13: The Art Side—AI Imagery 180

- The RunwayML Rabbit Hole

- Finding Your Visual Style with AI

- Prompts That Pop Off the Screen

- Image Editing Tricks That Actually Work

- Screenshot-Worthy Projects

- How to Make Stuff People *Want* to Share

Chapter 14: Where It Sneaks Into My Routine 292

- My AI-Powered Morning Routine

- Smart Shopping, Smarter Planning

- Note-Taking and Brain Dumps

- Quick Fixes for Random Problems

- Using Voice Tools Like a Podcast Pro

- My Week of Living Like a Bot (It Was Weird)

Chapter 15: The Future of My Creative Soul 203

- What's Coming in 2025 and Beyond

- Tools I'm Dying to Try

- Trends You Should Totally Watch

- Finding My Community of Nerdy Dreamers

- How I Plan to Keep Growing (Even with Robots Around)

Chapter 16: The AI Unleashed Survival Kit 215

- The Greatest Hits (Recap Time)

- Prompt Bank: My Secret Stash

- Mini Challenges for Your First Month

- Final Words Before You Go Create

Introduction: This Isn't a Book About Robots

You didn't pick up this book because you wanted to become an engineer. You're not here for an AI degree or a lecture on machine learning. You're here because something in you still wants to make things. Weird things. Wonderful things. Maybe you've got a notebook full of half-finished ideas, a Canva folder of maybe-brands, or a project you've been "about to start" since the pandemic.

Good news: this book is your creative permission slip, with AI as your co-conspirator.

This isn't about outsourcing your imagination. It's about *amplifying it*. About using new tools to spark new ideas, break past your own perfectionism, and finally create stuff that feels like *you*—but faster, weirder, and more fun.

You don't need to know how any of it works under the hood. You just need a little curiosity and a browser. And maybe a half-charged laptop, a cozy playlist, and something caffeinated nearby.

Inside these pages, you'll find:

- Ridiculously simple tools that generate art, stories, songs, and ideas in seconds

- Prompts that push you out of creative autopilot and into that "OMG I need to make this" feeling

- Hacks that make starting easier and finishing... possible (finally)

There are no rules here. No gatekeeping. No vibe police. Just you, your messy brilliance, and a set of AI tools that are about to become your favorite creative wing man. You don't need to be a "tech person." You just need to be the kind of person who still gets excited about ideas. You're not behind. You're not late. You're right on time.

Let's make some beautiful chaos.

Chapter 1: The AI Creative Party (And You're the Guest of Honor)

So you've heard the rumors. Robots are taking over, AI is replacing everyone, and your neighbor's dog is selling AI-generated NFTs. Sounds dramatic, right? But here's the twist. While the world panics over job losses and creepy robot overlords, there's this unexpected little movement growing fast. It's full of curious, creative people who aren't scared of AI. They're playing with it. And having a blast.

Welcome to the creative side of AI. It's wild, unpredictable, and way more fun than it sounds. Think of this chapter as your invite to a house party where everyone's experimenting with tools that can write stories, paint wild visuals, remix music, and throw out ideas that make you raise an eyebrow in the best way. No need for a tech background. You don't have to speak code. If you've got a Wi-Fi signal and even a sliver of curiosity, you belong here.

This isn't a textbook. It's more like a backstage pass to a creativity rave where the DJ happens to be artificial intelligence.

By the time you finish this book, you'll know how to team up with AI like it's your creative sidekick. You'll brainstorm faster, make cooler stuff, and finally finish that one idea you've been sitting on for two years. But before we get deep into prompts and platforms, I want to show you what's possible. I want you to feel that moment when the lightbulb goes off and you realize this stuff isn't just hype.

If you've ever stared at a blank page with no clue what to write. If you've wanted to create art but felt like your hands couldn't keep up with your imagination. If you've dreamed of turning a side idea into something real. This book is for you.

So grab a drink, kick your shoes off, and get comfortable. The creative energy is buzzing and the lights just dimmed. You're not here to study AI. You're here to play with it.

Ready? Let's go.

My First Time with AI (Spoiler: I Was Hooked)

I didn't plan to fall in love with artificial intelligence. It started, like most unexpectedly fun things, during a late-night scroll through the internet. I had just rage-quit a writing project that was draining the life out of me. The kind of writing that feels like pulling splinters from your brain. I was somewhere between procrastination and desperation when I saw this headline: *"This AI can write anything. Try it."*

Of course I clicked.

The site was simple. Just a blank text box that said, *"Ask me anything."* So naturally, I typed the first ridiculous thing that came to mind. I wrote, *"Write a breakup text from a pirate to a mermaid."* Don't ask me why. I was tired and slightly unhinged from too much coffee and not enough joy.

Then it answered.

Ah, me heart.
I be torn like sails in a storm. Yer song be sweet, but I belong to the sea. May the tides bring ye joy, even if it ain't with me.
Always yours,
Captain Hooked

I nearly dropped my phone from laughing. This thing had personality. It was clever. And more importantly, it made me want to keep going. I asked for more. A song about sad robots. A product pitch for invisible socks. The opening line of a mystery novel set in a haunted juice bar.

Within an hour, I had ten new ideas, half a short story, and a grin I hadn't worn in weeks.

What surprised me wasn't just how smart it seemed. It was how fast I started feeling creative again. This wasn't a tool that did the work for me. It was like a partner who never got tired, never judged my ideas, and never said no. I could toss out the weirdest thought, and it would run with it. It made me want to make stuff again.

Over the next few days, I started testing it with real things. Social captions. Slogans. Blog titles. It wasn't perfect, but neither am I. The difference was that this thing gave me momentum. And sometimes momentum is all you need to turn a blank page into something alive.

That was the moment I knew. This wasn't just another tech fad. It was a creative cheat code for people like me. People who have big ideas but sometimes get stuck translating them. People who think faster than they type. People who want to make cool things but don't want to spend hours stuck in their own heads.

So yeah. I was hooked. Not because AI was doing the work for me. But because it reminded me how fun creating could be when you're not doing it alone.

No Tech Degree? No Problem

Let's get one thing out of the way. You don't need to know a single line of code to use AI. Not one. You won't be asked to install Python, troubleshoot JavaScript errors, or explain what an algorithm is. If you can type a sentence, you're already qualified.

I know what it feels like to look at new tech and assume it's not for you. It's like walking into a gym full of people lifting tires and flipping ropes while you're still trying to figure out which direction the treadmill faces. That's how AI looked to me at first— cold, complicated, and full of buzzwords I didn't understand.

But that's not what modern AI tools are like. At least not the ones built for creators.

The new wave of AI platforms is built for everyday people who just want to get things done. Artists. Writers. Hustlers. Curious humans with no patience for tech snobbery. These tools are fast, intuitive, and most importantly, forgiving. You can mess up and still get something amazing out of them.

When I first opened an AI writing tool, it felt like texting a really smart, slightly unhinged friend. You don't need to use special language. You don't have to get it perfect. You just ask. Something like, "Give me ten names for a cozy mystery podcast." Or "Help me write a breakup letter from a ghost." That's it. The tool takes your idea and runs with it.

The first time you see it work, it almost feels like cheating. But it's not cheating. It's just a shortcut past the part where you doubt yourself.

This is a big mental shift for a lot of people. We're used to thinking that creativity should be hard. That unless you suffer for your art, it doesn't count. But what if you didn't have to struggle through every idea alone? What if your tools could meet you halfway?

AI doesn't replace your creativity. It gives it room to breathe.

That's why it doesn't matter if you've never built an app or touched Photoshop in your life. Some of the most creative people I've seen using these tools are the ones who come from zero technical background. They're teachers. Bartenders. Stay-at-home parents. Dancers. Crafters. Poets. None of them would describe themselves as "tech-savvy," but they all figured it out.

Why? Because these tools reward curiosity, not credentials.

In fact, not being a tech expert might be your secret advantage. You're not locked into a certain way of thinking. You don't care about syntax or system design. You care about whether the thing looks good. Whether the words hit. Whether the vibe is right. And when you're driven by instinct instead of instruction manuals, you end up making work that feels fresh and human.

A lot of hardcore tech folks get stuck trying to optimize everything. Creatives, on the other hand, know when to follow the weird idea. That's where the fun lives.

Don't get me wrong, there's value in learning more about how AI works under the hood. But that's extra credit. For now, just showing up and playing around is more than enough. You'll learn as you go, the same way you learned how to use a phone or ride a bike. It's clumsy at first, but then it clicks.

So here's the only real skill you need: the ability to ask questions. That's it. Curious questions. Funny questions. Questions that sound like you. The more you practice, the more you'll realize you already have what it takes. You're not here to become an engineer. You're here to unlock something that's already inside you.

No degree. No gatekeeping. Just your own brain, a little time, and an open mind. That's the ticket in.

What You'll Find in These Pages

This isn't a textbook. It's more like a creative survival guide, a stash of hacks, and a hype session rolled into one. You're not here to memorize anything. You're here to mess around, discover what clicks, and start making things you're proud of. If you finish this book and your head is buzzing with ideas, I'll consider it a win.

Let me give you a sneak peek into what's ahead.

First, we're going to talk about how AI actually helps your brain—not just in theory, but in a very real, "Wow, I didn't know I could do that" kind of way. If you've ever been stuck in creative quicksand, you'll see how AI can throw you a rope. It's not just a productivity booster. It's a perspective shifter.

Then we'll dig into the tools. And don't worry, I won't throw you into the deep end. Every tool in this book is something I've personally used, broken, misunderstood, fixed, and now genuinely love. Most of them are free. Many are ridiculously easy to use. I'll walk you through what each one does and show you what it looks like in action. Think of it like a behind-the-scenes tour, but without the boring parts.

You'll get walk-throughs for writing, art, music, brainstorming, and even some weird little side hustles that I swear people are actually making money from. You'll also get access to my favorite prompts—the ones I go back to again and again because they unlock something wild almost every time.

But this isn't just a "how to" book. It's also about mindset. We're going to talk about fear, imposter syndrome, burnout, and the myth that you have to suffer for your creativity. Spoiler alert: you don't. There's a better way. A more playful way. AI helps you rediscover the part of you that makes stuff just because it's fun.

Every chapter ends with something practical. You'll find prompts, mini challenges, or quick ideas you can try right away. You don't have to do them all, but they're there to keep the momentum going. I'm a big believer in action over perfection. Try first, judge later. Actually, don't judge at all. This is your playground. There are no rules.

You'll also see stories. Some are mine. Some are mashed-up versions of people I know. All of them are here to show you what's possible. These aren't stories about overnight success or viral fame. They're about little wins. The kind that make you sit up straighter and think, "Wait, I made that?"

This book is for the non-tech crowd. The daydreamers. The notebook scribblers. The people who love to create but sometimes need a push. You don't need to impress anyone. You just need to show up. Everything else, we'll figure out together.

By the end of this journey, you'll have your own set of tools. Your own go-to prompts. Your own weird habits that help you get unstuck. You'll know what kind of creative work feels like home to you, and you'll have a map for making more of it.

And maybe, just maybe, you'll start to see yourself differently. Not just as someone who dabbles or dreams, but as someone who makes things. Big things, small things, messy things, brilliant things. All powered by a tool that most people are still too scared to try.

But you? You said yes.

So turn the page. The good stuff starts now.

Who This Book Is Actually For

Let's be honest. Most books about AI feel like they were written for people who already own three monitors and drink protein shakes while coding at 2 a.m. That's not you. Or if it is, you might still want a break from the jargon. This book isn't for the engineers or the data scientists. It's for everyone else.

It's for the artists who feel like their sketchbook hasn't seen sunlight in months. The writers who have a Google Doc full of unfinished ideas and abandoned titles. The side-hustlers trying to name a product, build a brand, or write a bio that doesn't sound like it was copied from someone's LinkedIn profile.

It's for the ones who used to be creative but somehow lost the spark. The ones who hear about AI tools and think, "That's probably cool but I wouldn't even know where to start." You're exactly the kind of person this book was written for.

You don't need to be tech-savvy. You don't need to have any experience with design software, editing programs, or writing apps. You just need to be willing to poke around and try things. That's it. If you can ask a question, you're already halfway there.

This book is also for people who love the idea of making stuff but get overwhelmed by the process. The blank page. The blinking cursor. The feeling that whatever you're about to make probably won't be good enough. AI helps you move past that. It gives you something to react to. Something to build on. It lowers the stakes so you can play more and panic less.

And hey, if you've ever thought you weren't the "creative type," I'm going to challenge that. Hard. You may not paint or write novels or design logos, but creativity is just your brain making connections. If you've ever rearranged furniture and felt proud of the result, you're creative. If you've made a playlist with a theme, you're creative. If you've told a joke, dreamed up a business name, doodled in a notebook, solved a weird problem at work, or come up with a new recipe, guess what. You're already doing the thing.

You don't need to change who you are to use AI. You just need to approach it the way you'd approach a new app or a new recipe. A little curiosity goes a long way. The tools are here, and they're better than ever. The only difference between you and someone already using them is that they gave themselves permission to try.

So whether you're looking for a new creative tool, a side hustle spark, or just something to shake up your routine, you're in the right place. This book won't turn you into a robot. It'll help you remember what it feels like to enjoy making things again.

You're not behind. You're not too late. You're exactly on time.

One Quick Win to Get You Hyped

Before we dive deeper into tools and techniques, I want you to try something. Right now. No prep, no overthinking. Just a simple prompt that shows how powerful this stuff can be when you actually give it a spin.

Go to your favorite AI writing tool. If you don't have one yet, open ChatGPT in your browser or find any other free AI platform that lets you type into a box and get a response. Don't worry if it looks intimidating. You're just going to write one line.

Here it is:

"Give me five story ideas where a totally ordinary person discovers something extraordinary by accident."

Now hit enter. Watch what happens.

You're probably going to see a list of scenarios that are weird, funny, dramatic, or strangely insightful. Maybe there's a janitor who finds a time-traveling mop. Or a retiree who starts hearing plants talk. Or a barista who accidentally invents a new language with their latte art. It doesn't matter if the results are brilliant or completely ridiculous. What matters is how fast they appear. That's the moment where most people sit back and go, "Oh. That was easy."

This is your quick win.

You didn't need a tutorial. You didn't need to study AI architecture. You just asked a question and got something back that sparked your imagination. That little spark is what we're chasing throughout this book. Not perfection. Not technical mastery. Just the spark.

Now take it one step further. Pick your favorite idea from the list. Doesn't matter which one. Then type:

"Write the opening paragraph of this story in a funny but dramatic tone."

Boom. You've got a beginning. Is it perfect? Probably not. But it's something you can work with. You're not starting from nothing. You're already in motion. And that's the point.

This is how you learn. This is how you unlock creative energy. One playful prompt at a time.

If you're feeling brave, tweak the prompt. Try a genre you usually avoid. Ask for ideas about aliens, or rom-coms, or detective squirrels. The more unexpected, the better. You don't have to show anyone what comes out. This is just for you. But if you do get something wild or wonderful, screenshot it. Save it. You'll be surprised how often one strange little idea can turn into something you want to build on.

The hardest part of any creative project is the beginning. The blank page has a way of staring back at you with judgment.

But when you're using AI, you're never starting from zero. You're jumping into something already moving. And movement leads to ideas.

If this little experiment made you smile, you're ready. If it made you laugh, even better. If it gave you a plot idea, a product name, or a character you can't stop thinking about, then you already know what's possible.

This is just the first step, but it's a big one.

Because now you've seen it.

You're not just reading about AI. You're using it. You're playing with it. You've taken your first step into a whole new creative space where you don't have to wait for inspiration. You can spark it yourself, any time you want.

And the best part? This is just the warm-up.

Chapter 2: Flipping the Creative Switch with AI

"Creativity is intelligence having fun."
— Albert Einstein

There's this moment that happens when you start using AI tools regularly. It's subtle, but powerful. You go from thinking of AI as a novelty to realizing it's actually changing the way your brain works. Not in a creepy, robot-implant kind of way. More like someone finally opened a few windows in your creative attic and let some fresh air in.

At first, you're just testing stuff. You try a few prompts, laugh at the results, maybe save something for later. But then you start noticing something weird. You're thinking in prompts throughout the day. You'll see a commercial and wonder how the AI would rewrite it. You'll overhear a conversation and think, *That would make a great opening scene.* You'll start catching your own mental patterns and flipping them for fun. And suddenly, you're not just consuming ideas. You're generating them.

This chapter is all about that switch. The mental shift from feeling stuck, bored, or creatively blocked to feeling like your brain is a bit more electric. Like your creative instincts are waking up again.

We'll look at why AI actually makes this easier, not harder. How it turns your brain into more of a collaborator than a critic. And why the science behind it might explain why you suddenly feel more inspired, even when you're just playing around.

Whether you're coming in with years of creative experience or just testing the waters, this is the part where the fun starts to feel a little more real. It's not about AI replacing your spark. It's about giving it fuel.

So if you've ever felt like your creativity was asleep at the wheel, consider this the moment where it starts hitting the gas.

My Lightbulb Moment That Changed Everything

It started with a deadline. Not the inspiring kind. The kind that lurks in your calendar for weeks, quietly judging you while you ignore it. I had a blog post due for a freelance gig, and I had absolutely nothing. No hook. No headline. No angle. Just a lot of pacing, sighing, and pretending to "think" while scrolling through unrelated tabs.

I wasn't new to writing. I'd done this kind of thing before, plenty of times. But for whatever reason, my brain felt like it had gone into power-saving mode. Every idea I wrote down felt tired. Every sentence sounded like a thousand others I'd written. I tried freewriting. I tried stepping away. I even tried making a snack, which somehow turned into reorganizing my spice cabinet. Still nothing.

Out of frustration, I opened ChatGPT and typed something half-hearted:

"Give me five angles for a blog post about staying creative when you're burned out."

What came back wasn't mind-blowing, but it was… useful. It gave me a few solid concepts, a few corny ones, and one that made me pause. *"The Creative Recharge: How to Make Space for Inspiration Without Quitting Your Day Job."* That one sparked something. Not because it was genius. But because it gave me somewhere to start.

I took that headline and asked for an outline. Then I asked for a few sentence starters. I ignored most of what came back, but a couple lines stuck. And suddenly, I wasn't stuck anymore. The wheels were turning. I started writing. Not copying, not pasting, just building. Shaping. Editing. The way I normally would, except this time, I wasn't frozen.

I finished the piece in just under two hours. And it was good. Not just passable. Not just "will do." It actually had personality. Humor. Flow. It felt like mine, because it *was* mine—I just didn't have to fight so hard to get it out.

That was the moment something clicked. It wasn't about getting perfect answers from the AI. It was about momentum. Movement. It gave me just enough to break the cycle of doubt and hesitation, and once I was in motion, the rest came naturally.

I realized then that AI wasn't my replacement. It was my warm-up. My brainstorming partner. My personal assistant who didn't care how many bad drafts I needed before I found a good one.

After that, I started using AI regularly—not for everything, but for the parts that used to slow me down. Naming things. Brainstorming titles. Writing the first terrible draft that I could later rewrite with confidence. The difference it made wasn't in the final product. It was in how fast I could get started.

I used to think creative breakthroughs only came in dramatic flashes. Like lightning strikes or 3 a.m. epiphanies. But most of the time, they're smaller than that. A good idea hiding in a list. A weird sentence that makes you laugh. A phrase that sparks a new angle. AI gives you more chances for those tiny breakthroughs, and it does it in seconds.

Now, whenever someone tells me they feel creatively blocked, I don't give advice. I give them a prompt.

Not every lightbulb moment feels like magic. Sometimes it feels like getting unstuck, just enough to remember that you actually like making things.

And that's more than enough.

Why Your Brain Loves a Bot

We like to imagine creativity as this mystical, emotional thing. Something that floats down from the clouds when the vibe is right. And sure, sometimes it feels that way. But most of the time? Creativity is just your brain making connections. One thought links to another, and eventually something weird or beautiful shows up.

The problem is that your brain isn't always in the mood. It overthinks. It stalls out. It gets caught in loops. It wants to be brilliant but also wants to avoid risk, failure, and looking like an idiot. That's where AI comes in.

AI doesn't think like us. And that's the magic.

Your brain loves novelty. It craves surprises. Even small ones. That's why a random word can spark a story, or a strange image can inspire a full-blown idea. When you interact with AI, it constantly throws unexpected responses at you. Not all of them are gold, but they keep your brain moving. They break the loop.

This is backed by science, by the way. Studies on creativity often link it to something called "divergent thinking." That's a fancy way of saying the ability to come up with lots of ideas, not just one good one. The more ideas you can generate, the more likely you are to hit something interesting.

AI is a divergent thinking machine. It doesn't get embarrassed by bad ideas. It doesn't pause to wonder if a pirate dating app is too niche. It just keeps going. And when you feed off that energy, your own mind starts loosening up. You stop filtering so hard. You start playing again.

Another brain-friendly benefit is speed. One of the biggest enemies of creativity is delay. The longer you sit with an empty page, the louder your self-doubt gets. But with AI, you ask a question and get a response in seconds. That instant feedback gives your brain something to work with. Even if it's off-topic or weird, it gives you momentum.

Momentum leads to flow. That sweet zone where time melts, your inner critic goes quiet, and you actually enjoy the process. Getting into flow is hard when you're forcing ideas. But it's way easier when you're reacting to something. That's what AI gives you—something to react to.

Let's not ignore another key factor: permission.

When you use AI, it feels like someone gave you permission to make something that doesn't have to be perfect. That's powerful. Most of us are walking around with creativity locked behind a wall of perfectionism. AI lowers that wall. It gives you something rough to shape, so you're not responsible for building the whole castle from scratch.

There's also this weird side effect I didn't expect. The more you use AI, the more confident you get with your own ideas. You start noticing patterns. You get better at giving prompts. You learn what sounds like you and what doesn't. Over time, you start to trust your own voice more—not less. Because now, you're in the driver's seat, and AI is just helping with directions.

That shift is everything.

So yes, your brain loves a bot. Not because it's trying to become one, but because the bot gives it room to stretch out. To explore. To take a break from the pressure and just follow the curiosity.

You don't need to know how the tech works. You don't need to understand the math behind machine learning. What matters is how it *feels* to use it. And if it feels easier, faster, lighter, more fun. that's a win.

We were never meant to do this alone. Not the writing. Not the drawing. Not the dreaming. Creativity has always been collaborative, even when it's just you and a notebook. Now you've got a new kind of partner. One that's ready whenever you are.

And that, scientifically speaking, is pretty damn cool.

Creativity vs. Overthinking (And How AI Helps)

Let's talk about the enemy of all good ideas. It's not lack of talent. It's not having the wrong tools. It's not even time. It's that voice in your head that overanalyzes everything before you even get started.

You know the one. You sit down to write or draw or brainstorm a name for your new thing, and your brain immediately jumps into critique mode. Is this good enough? Does this make sense? Has this been done before? Will people think it's weird? What if it's boring? What if it flops?

That voice is loud. It's persistent. And it's very good at convincing you to do nothing.

Overthinking is a creativity killer. It doesn't usually show up as full-blown anxiety. It sneaks in quietly. You open a document and feel the need to outline everything before you type. You sketch a shape and erase it five times. You write a line, delete it, and spend fifteen minutes reworking a sentence that doesn't even matter. That's not refining. That's stalling.

What makes it worse is that creative people are often perfectionists in disguise. You want the idea to come out fully formed. You want it to be clever, polished, and impressive right from the start. But that's not how ideas are born. They're messy. They need space to be weird before they get good.

This is where AI comes in like a wrecking ball. In the best way.

When you use an AI tool to generate ideas, outlines, headlines, sketches, or even random nonsense, you bypass the need to get it right on the first try. You're no longer starting from a blank page. You're responding. That tiny shift—from creation to collaboration—breaks the overthinking loop.

Instead of debating whether your idea is good enough to start, you just start. You tell the AI to give you ten ideas. You pick one. You tweak it. You rewrite the parts that don't fit. You add your own flavor. You stay in motion, and that's what matters.

The longer you stare at a blank screen, the louder that inner critic gets. But when you ask an AI for help, the screen fills up fast. And even if what comes back is weird or off, it gets you thinking. It sparks something. Suddenly, you're shaping instead of struggling.

Another reason AI helps with overthinking is that it doesn't judge. You can ask it the weirdest questions without feeling self-conscious. You don't have to worry about being wrong or sounding silly. There's no pressure. That freedom makes it easier to experiment, and experimentation is where all good ideas begin.

Here's a trick I use when I feel stuck. I'll type something like, "Write the worst opening line to a novel ever written." The result is usually hilarious and ridiculous, and that breaks the tension. Then I'll type, "Now write a better version of that same line, but make it feel mysterious." That little game gets me moving without stress. It's not about brilliance. It's about flow.

You can do the same thing with visuals, music, taglines, product names, or even social captions. Ask the AI to give you something bad on purpose. Laugh at it. Then improve it. You'll be surprised how much easier it is to create once you give yourself permission to start ugly.

The biggest lie overthinking tells you is that you need to be ready before you begin. The truth is, beginning is what gets you ready. Movement leads to momentum. And momentum silences doubt faster than any pep talk ever could.

With AI, you don't have to wait for inspiration to strike. You can generate it on demand. You can trick your brain into starting by removing the pressure to be original, smart, or perfect. You just need to ask a question.

The more you do this, the more confident you'll get. You'll stop second-guessing yourself so much. You'll trust your instincts more. You'll remember that creativity is supposed to feel good, not stressful.

AI doesn't just help you make things. It helps you *keep* making things. Even on the days when your brain is working against you.

That's not cheating. That's smart.

Weird but True: Science Behind AI Imagination

It's a little strange to say that AI can be imaginative. After all, it doesn't have feelings. It doesn't dream. It doesn't grow up doodling spaceships in the margins of math worksheets. But somehow, when you give it the right nudge, it churns out stuff that feels weirdly creative.

So what's actually going on?

AI doesn't imagine the way humans do. It doesn't close its eyes and picture a pink elephant riding a unicycle through Times Square. What it does instead is pattern recognition. A lot of it. When you give it a prompt, it searches through an enormous network of patterns it has seen before, rearranging pieces of language, imagery, or logic into something that fits your request.

The result? Something new. Or at least something that feels new to you.

This is where it gets interesting. Creativity in humans isn't magic either. It's actually not that far off from what AI is doing. Your brain also thrives on patterns. When you create, you're pulling together memories, words, images, ideas, sounds, and emotions. You're remixing things you've seen, heard, or felt before. AI just does it at a much faster scale.

The brain has a region called the default mode network. It's the part that lights up when your mind is wandering, daydreaming, or connecting seemingly unrelated dots. Some researchers believe this is where creativity gets its spark. It's not a logical process. It's messy, nonlinear, and fueled by subconscious associations.

AI has no default mode network. It doesn't get inspired or distracted or emotionally invested. But it mimics some of the effects. When you give it an open-ended question or a bizarre prompt, it scrambles to generate something that fits, often pulling together connections you wouldn't have made on your own.

It's like handing your brain a box of puzzle pieces you didn't know existed.

That's why the results can feel strangely insightful. Not because the AI understands the idea, but because your brain does.

You see something unexpected, and your brain lights up. You start to see possibilities. You start filling in the blanks.

This is why collaboration with AI feels less artificial and more like a strange conversation. It gives you back raw material, and your brain adds the meaning. You decide what's worth shaping, what sparks a new thought, what deserves a second look. That blend of logic and intuition, machine speed and human feeling, is what makes it powerful.

And sometimes, the randomness is part of the charm.

There's a theory in neuroscience called stochastic resonance. In simple terms, it means that a little bit of noise in a system can actually improve performance. That randomness helps us notice things we wouldn't otherwise pick up. AI brings in just enough randomness to nudge your brain out of its usual path.

Let's say you're trying to write a story and keep defaulting to the same old character types. You ask the AI for a character, and it gives you a lonely beekeeper who moonlights as an amateur ghost hunter. Now your brain is cooking. Even if you don't use that exact idea, you've been bumped off the familiar path and landed somewhere new.

You don't have to understand the science to benefit from it. But it's nice to know that what feels magical actually has a structure behind it. You're not just getting lucky. You're tapping into a very real interaction between your brain's creative machinery and the algorithm's endless supply of surprise.

The goal isn't to make AI feel human. The goal is to make *you* feel more creative when you use it.

That's the sweet spot.

So the next time your brain feels flat, feed it a little chaos. Ask the AI something off the wall. Something your inner critic would normally shoot down. You might not use the answer, but you'll almost definitely feel something shift.

That little shift is where all good ideas begin.

Quick Wins to Try Right Now

Let's keep the momentum going. You've read about how AI can help you think differently, unlock ideas, and escape the spiral of overthinking. Now it's time to test it out for yourself.

You don't need to block off an afternoon or light a candle to summon the muses. These are short, simple exercises designed to give you a taste of what's possible. Each one takes five minutes or less. The goal isn't perfection. It's movement.

You ready? Let's go.

1. Idea Storm: Remix Edition

Open your AI writing tool of choice. Type in this prompt:

"Give me ten ridiculous business ideas that sound like they could actually work."

Read through the list. Pick one that makes you laugh, raise an eyebrow, or say, "That's dumb, but kind of brilliant." Now ask:

"Write a short product description for this idea as if it already exists."

Boom. You've just gone from zero to concept in under three minutes.

2. Image Prompt Playground

If you're using an AI art generator like DALL·E or any image tool, try this:

"A cat dressed as a detective solving crimes in a neon city, cinematic style."

You can swap the subject, setting, or vibe. Go cute, go weird, go epic. Just watch what happens. You'll get something visual you never would've thought to draw yourself. It doesn't have to be good. It just has to be surprising.

3. Soundtrack Spark

Using an AI music generator? Ask it to create:

"A theme song for a superhero who can only use their powers on Tuesdays."

Now close your eyes and imagine the movie trailer that would go with it. Even if you're not a musician, you're still creating something new. That's the point.

4. Word Flip Challenge

Type this into your AI tool:

"Take this sentence and rewrite it five different ways with totally different tones: 'I forgot my lunch at home.'"

You'll start to see how tone changes everything. Then try writing your own sentence and repeat the process. This builds your voice and makes you more confident in how you say what you want to say.

5. The Unexpected Muse

This one is strange, but trust me. Ask your AI:

"What would a cloud say if it wrote a journal entry about its day?"

Now read the answer and respond to it. Write back like it's a pen pal. Don't worry if it makes sense. The act of responding to something unusual is enough to shake your creative brain awake.

6. The "Bad First Draft" Trick

Start with something messy on purpose. Ask the AI:

"Write the worst opening line for a fantasy novel involving dragons and coffee."

Once you stop laughing, ask:

"Now write a better version that still includes both dragons and coffee."

This gets your brain into a playful state, which is way better than staring at a blinking cursor waiting for genius to appear.

7. Journal with a Twist

Ask the AI to give you five journal prompts based on the theme "reinvention." Pick one, write for two minutes, then ask the AI to expand on what you wrote or ask you a follow-up question. Suddenly, you're not journaling alone. You're in a dialogue with something that's helping you go deeper.

You don't have to try all of these. Even one can spark something unexpected. The point is to stop thinking about using AI and actually *use* it. No overthinking, no pressure. Just play. If one of these sparks a new idea, run with it. Save it. Share it. Build on it. And if it doesn't? Cool. You tried something. That's a win in itself.

Creativity isn't about waiting for inspiration. It's about learning how to tap into it, even when you don't feel ready. These exercises are like jumper cables for your brain. Next time you feel stuck, come back to this page. Pick one. Light the spark.

You're officially out of neutral.

Chapter 3: My Favorite Free AI Tools (You're Welcome)

By now, you're probably thinking, "Okay, this all sounds great, but how do I actually do it?" You're ready to click something, type something, maybe even make something. Good news: this is the part where I hand you the keys.

The next few sections are a tour of my favorite free AI tools. These aren't just random apps I found while googling at 2 a.m. I've used all of them. I've tested their limits, broken them a few times, and even managed to make something I was proud of using nothing but a weird idea and an internet connection.

These tools are simple enough for beginners, but powerful enough to grow with you. Most of them don't even require sign-ups, and if they do, it's the kind where you give them your email and they give you magic in return. No credit card, no trial that charges you on day eight, no strings.

You're not going to get buried in technical setup here. I'm not here to turn you into a machine whisperer. I'm here to help you get inspired fast and start making things even faster. Whether you're into writing, visual art, sound design, or just pure idea generation, there's something in here for you.

And if you're already familiar with a few of these, don't skip ahead. I'll show you new ways to use them that you might not have tried yet. Sometimes it's not the tool—it's how you use it. This is your digital treasure chest. Crack it open, take what you need, and come back whenever you want to play.

Let's start with the fun stuff.

The Treasure Chest You Didn't Know Existed

Most people think AI tools are locked behind paywalls, subscriptions, or complicated software that only engineers can understand. But the truth is, we're living in a golden age of free tools that are insanely powerful and surprisingly easy to use.

If you've ever opened Photoshop and immediately closed it out of fear, or stared at a blank Google Doc wondering how people write thousands of words, you're about to feel very seen—and very relieved.

There's a whole collection of AI tools just sitting out there waiting to be used. Think of them as digital power-ups. Each one gives you a different kind of superpower. Some help you write faster. Others generate wild visuals from a single sentence. Some can make music, remix your voice, or spit out business ideas you'd never think of on your own.

The best part? You don't need a dime to use most of them. No trials. No hidden fees. Just open the site, type something in, and watch the magic happen.

Let's start with a few examples.

ChatGPT

This is the one you've probably already heard about. It's a conversational AI that responds to prompts in a human-like way. You can ask it to brainstorm blog ideas, write song lyrics, fix your grammar, or help you plot a story about a time-traveling sandwich. It's flexible, fast, and way smarter than it has any right to be. Best of all, the free version is usually more than enough for what you'll want to do.

Craiyon (formerly DALL·E Mini)

This tool generates images based on text prompts. Want a penguin dressed like a pirate holding a balloon? Type it in. You'll get nine hilariously strange images that feel like your imagination came to life after a shot of espresso. It's not always polished, but it's fun, fast, and addictively weird.

RunwayML

This one's a little more advanced, but still friendly to beginners. It lets you create videos, edit content, remove backgrounds, and even generate animations—all with AI. It's like a creative lab built for people who want professional-looking results without professional-level skills. The free tier gives you just enough to experiment and get hooked.

Tome

Tome is like a presentation wizard. You give it an idea, and it creates an entire slide deck—images, layout, and even text. Perfect if you're pitching an idea, starting a brand, or just want to see how far you can stretch a concept with minimal effort.

Soundraw and Beatoven

These are AI music generators. You pick a mood, tempo, and genre, and they generate original music you can use in videos, podcasts, or creative projects. No music background required. You just click and jam.

And that's barely scratching the surface.

There are tools that generate voices, tools that write poetry, tools that build websites, and tools that help you practice languages. The internet is full of these little digital machines quietly waiting to make your life easier, cooler, and more creative.

So why haven't more people jumped in?

Most people don't know where to look. Or they assume it's all expensive, hard to learn, or only useful for tech people. That's what makes this feel like a treasure chest. The tools are out there. You just need someone to show you where to dig.

That's what the rest of this chapter is for. I'm going to walk you through my favorites, show you what they're good at, and give you ideas for how to use them. You don't have to memorize anything. Just skim, click, and try whatever sounds fun. The whole point is to explore.

Because once you get your hands on these tools, something shifts. You stop thinking about creativity as this slow, lonely process. It starts to feel fast, playful, and kind of addictive in the best way.

There's no secret password. No membership required. Just curiosity, a browser, and maybe a decent cup of coffee.

You're in.

AI Tools That Feel Like Magic

Some tools are useful. Others are cool. But every once in a while, you stumble onto something that makes you stop, blink twice, and say out loud, "Wait, how is this even real?"

That's what this section is all about. These are the tools that feel like magic. The ones that make you grin like a kid with a new toy. You don't need any experience to use them. Just an idea, a few words, or a wild question. They do the rest.

Let's take a look at a few that made me do a double take the first time I used them.

ChatGPT

Yes, we're talking about it again because it's that good. It doesn't just respond to questions. It plays along. It writes poems, summarizes dense articles, answers awkward questions, and helps you brainstorm names for your dog grooming side hustle. Ask it to explain quantum physics in the voice of a pirate. It will. Ask it to rewrite your bio like it's the back cover of a romance novel. Done. It feels like having a creative partner who's always online and never tired.

DALL·E

Not the mini version this time. The full DALL·E (if you can get access or use it through platforms like Bing Image Creator) takes your words and turns them into surprisingly polished artwork. You can describe a scene in detail, and within seconds it generates a set of visuals that feel like concept art from a movie you didn't know you wanted to see. It is especially fun for imagining characters, creating surreal visuals, or mocking up ideas you could never draw on your own.

RunwayML's Text to Video Tool

You type a short phrase like "a glowing jellyfish floating through space" and it creates an actual video clip. It is short, yes, and a little rough around the edges. But it looks like something that came out of a sci-fi short film. This is the kind of tool that gives you chills the first time you use it because you can immediately see where this is going. And where it is going is wild.

Tome

Imagine you are pitching a new product idea and you want a slick presentation in five minutes or less. You open Tome, give it a sentence or two about your concept, and it builds an entire slide deck with visuals, layout, and copy. It is the kind of thing that would take someone hours in PowerPoint or Canva, and it does it in seconds. If you have a business brain, this tool will make you feel like you have a design team in your pocket.

Soundraw

Here's one for the music lovers. Soundraw lets you generate original music by picking a genre, mood, and tempo. It builds a full song for you, complete with different sections like intro, chorus, and bridge. You can tweak each part, change the vibe, and even download tracks to use in your projects. Whether you are making videos, podcasts, or just want a custom soundtrack for your creative flow, this tool feels like magic in headphone form.

These tools are easy to try and even easier to get hooked on. What makes them feel magical isn't just the output, it is the speed. The moment between "I wonder what would happen if..." and actually seeing it happen is so short that your brain barely has time to overthink. That gap, or lack of one, is where creativity thrives.

You are no longer imagining something and then waiting forever to see if it works. You try it, see it, and adjust in real time.

It creates a feedback loop that keeps you moving forward. That is why these tools are so powerful. They remove the friction between idea and execution.

You don't have to be good at this. You just have to be curious. The magic happens when you let go of the need to be impressive and lean into the joy of experimenting. These aren't just apps or websites. They are doors. Each one opens into a new room of your creativity you didn't know existed.

So go knock. Better yet, kick it open.

Free Beats Paid (Most of the Time)

One of the biggest myths about creative tools is that you need to pay up to get anything decent. Premium memberships, pro plans, monthly subscriptions, upsells at every corner. It can feel like there is a velvet rope around all the good stuff.

The truth? You can do a lot with free. Way more than you might think.

I've used dozens of AI tools at this point. Some with fancy features that come with a price tag, others that are totally open to anyone. And I can say this with full confidence. You do not need to spend a single dollar to start creating cool things.

Most of the tools I use every week are free, or at least offer a strong free tier. The kind that actually lets you do meaningful work without nagging you every five minutes to upgrade. These tools are not watered down. They are powerful, fast, and more than enough to help you build momentum.

Take ChatGPT. The free version handles most creative prompts like a champ. Whether you are writing, brainstorming, or tweaking copy, you can get 90 percent of the value without ever paying for the upgraded model. Sure, the paid version is a bit sharper and better at nuance, but for most people, that difference is not a dealbreaker.

Same goes for image generators like Craiyon or Bing Image Creator. You might not get ultra high resolution or perfect lighting, but what you do get is plenty to inspire, visualize, and even use in projects. And honestly, some of the weird glitches just make things more fun.

Even RunwayML, which has paid tiers, lets you experiment for free. You can remove video backgrounds, try out motion effects, and create short clips. It is not unlimited, but it gives you enough to learn and test ideas before you ever spend a dime.

The trick is knowing how to stretch the tools. Think like a creative problem solver. If one platform hits a wall, combine it with another. Maybe you use one AI to write a script and another to turn it into images. Maybe you edit your visuals in a separate free tool like Canva. Stack your resources. That is the beauty of the internet right now. Everything connects.

Another reason to stick with free tools at the start is freedom. When you are not paying for something, you are more willing to experiment. There is no pressure to get your money's worth. You can try bold, weird ideas. You can make mistakes. You can ditch one tool and try another without guilt.

That sense of play is where the best ideas come from. And it is harder to access when you are constantly calculating value per month.

Now, that's not to say all paid tools are bad or unnecessary. Some are absolutely worth it once you hit a certain point. If you start selling your work, building a brand, or working with clients, it might make sense to upgrade. Premium features can unlock more precision, faster outputs, or better customization. But that is a decision for later.

Right now, the goal is to build creative muscle without burning a hole in your wallet.

The only investment you need to make at this stage is time. And even that is a light ask. These tools are designed for speed. You can get results in seconds, test variations in minutes, and build a portfolio in days. You do not need a subscription to do that. You just need curiosity and a willingness to play.

So before you sign up for anything, start with what is free. Push it. Mix it. Break it a little. See how far you can go on zero dollars.

You will be surprised how far that actually is.

Setup So Simple It's Silly

Let's clear something up right now. You don't need to install anything. You don't need to wire anything together. You won't be looking at a blank terminal screen with blinking code. Getting started with AI tools is easier than making toast. If you can open a browser and type into a box, you are already overqualified.

I say this because I know how intimidating it can feel when you first hear about AI platforms. Words like API, neural networks, and cloud infrastructure sound like they belong in a tech conference, not in your creative toolkit. But you don't need to know any of that.

Most of the tools I've talked about work straight from your browser. No downloads, no configurations, no special devices. Just visit the website, type your idea, and press go.

Let's walk through what it usually looks like.

Step one: Pick a tool

Decide what you want to do. Do you want to write something? Try

ChatGPT. Want an image? Head to Craiyon or Bing Image Creator. Need music? Soundraw has you covered. Whatever you are curious about, there's probably a free tool that already does it.

Step two: Visit the site

Open your browser and type in the tool's name. Most of them will show up right away in search. Click the official link and you are in.

Step three: Start typing

There is usually a blank prompt box with a little bit of guidance nearby. Don't worry if you don't know what to say. Just start with something simple like, "Write a poem about a dragon who loves pizza," or "Create an image of a futuristic city underwater." Then click generate.

Step four: React

This is where the fun begins. You will see results within seconds. If it is close to what you want, keep building on it. If it is way off, change your prompt and try again. This back-and-forth is where you start learning what works best. It is like learning how to talk to a new creative partner who never gets tired of your wild ideas.

There is no secret trick to becoming good at this. The tools are designed to be used by regular people. That means you do not need a tutorial or a walkthrough every time. You just need to be willing to experiment. And since you are not installing anything or setting up complex accounts, there is no risk. If you hate the results, just close the tab. That's it.

And here is something even better. A lot of these tools now come with built-in templates or examples. That means you do not have to start from scratch. You can browse what other people are making, remix their prompts, or use them as inspiration for your own ideas. It is like walking into a workshop where everyone is building cool stuff and you get to peek over their shoulders.

The simplicity of setup is part of the magic. You do not waste time fumbling through menus or watching endless setup tutorials. You just create. Even when a site asks for sign-up, it is usually quick and painless. You toss in an email, maybe confirm with a code, and you are good to go. No waiting for approvals, no hidden fees, no weird downloads sitting on your desktop.

So if you have been holding back because you thought AI was too complicated, this is your moment. Take that first click. You are not committing to anything. You are just trying it out.

What you will find is that the hardest part is not the tech. It is getting over the idea that it is not for you.

But now you know better. You are already capable of using these tools. And not just using them, but creating something with them that feels personal, exciting, and actually fun.

The setup? It's just typing. You've been training for this your whole life.

Tool Taste Test

You've met the tools. Now let's use them. This is where theory becomes play, and curiosity turns into momentum. Think of this section as your guided sandbox. We're going to walk through simple ways to test-drive each tool so you can get real results in under ten minutes per experiment. You don't need to commit to anything. Just try things. Break things. See what feels good.

Let's jump in.

1. ChatGPT: Idea Jam with Style

Head to chat.openai.com and create a free account if you don't already have one. Once you're in, you'll see a blank chat window waiting for your prompt. Start by typing:

"Give me five unusual blog post ideas about boredom and creativity."

After you hit enter, read through the list. Pick one that feels interesting or makes you laugh. Now ask:

"Write the first paragraph of that blog post in a casual, witty tone."

The AI will respond right away. Read it. Does it sound like something you'd keep writing? If not, ask it to rewrite the same paragraph but make it more dramatic, or more poetic, or more sarcastic. Keep tinkering. This is where the magic happens—not in getting the perfect response on the first try, but in shaping something that starts to sound like you.

2. Craiyon: Word-to-Image Wizardry

Go to www.craiyon.com. You'll see a simple search box at the top of the page. In that box, type:

"A jellyfish floating through a neon city at night, cinematic lighting, digital art style."

Click "Draw" and wait about a minute while the tool generates nine different interpretations. They might be surreal, funny, or a little glitchy. Pick one that catches your eye. If none do, slightly adjust your prompt. Try changing "neon city" to "desert highway" or "underwater castle." You can then download your favorite result or use it as visual inspiration for a writing or design project.

3. RunwayML: Instant Video Magic

Visit www.runwayml.com and create a free account. Once you're logged in, head to the "AI Magic Tools" section. Choose "Remove Background" or "Text to Image." For this walkthrough, let's try Remove Background.

Click the tool, then upload a short video clip. You can use their sample footage if you don't have anything handy. Once uploaded, the tool will automatically remove the background, leaving your subject in place. From here, you can export the video or bring it into a different app for editing. Try layering it over a new background or adding text. See how far you can go with just a few clicks.

4. Tome: Instant Presentation Builder

Head over to www.tome.app and sign up with Google or email. Once you're in, click "New Tome" to start your first presentation. In the box, write something like:

"Create a pitch deck for a fictional board game called 'Dinner With Vampires.' The game is about surviving awkward meals with undead relatives."

Within seconds, Tome will generate slides that include titles, subheadings, copy, and images. Flip through the slides. If the tone isn't what you want, ask it to regenerate the content with a specific style like "funny and playful" or "professional startup tone." You can edit the layout or tweak the text directly. Even if it's silly, this exercise shows how fast you can go from idea to pitch without designing anything yourself.

5. Soundraw: Your Personal Music Generator

Visit www.soundraw.io and try the free demo. You don't need to log in yet. On the homepage, you'll see a genre and mood selector. Choose something like "Lofi" and then select "Relaxed" or "Dreamy" as your mood. Click "Create Music" and listen to the track that appears.

Now click "Edit" on the song. You can rearrange parts, extend the chorus, or mute instruments. Try adjusting the tempo or swapping out the lead instrument to change the vibe completely. If you're working on a video, podcast, or writing session, download the track and use it as your soundtrack. Even if you don't normally mess with music, this shows how accessible sound design can be.

You don't need to do all of these today. Start with one or two. Pick the one that sparks the most curiosity. Save what you create. Screenshot it. Write about how it made you feel. Share it with a friend, or just admire the fact that you made something out of thin air.

The point isn't to master the tools. It's to start using them without fear. Every click builds your creative muscles. Every experiment gives you a better sense of what's possible. This is your toolkit now. Not something to study from a distance, but something to play with. You're not waiting for permission. You're already creating.

And you haven't even hit your stride yet.

Chapter 4: Writing with AI — My Words, Its Wings

Writing is personal. It is messy, emotional, and sometimes weirdly hard to start. Even if you have ideas bubbling in your brain, turning them into something on the page can feel like wrestling a cloud. That is why so many people get stuck at the beginning. They know what they want to say, but that blinking cursor becomes a silent judge.

AI changes that.

This chapter is not about giving your voice away. It is about amplifying it. You are still the writer. You are still the one with the story, the feeling, the purpose. The difference is, now you have a tool that can help you get there faster. Or get you unstuck. Or throw you a curveball you didn't see coming.

Writing with AI is not about letting a machine do the talking. It is about having a sidekick that never runs out of energy. One that can brainstorm with you, write rough drafts, generate headlines, clean up clunky sentences, or help you figure out what your next paragraph could be. You still make the decisions. You still guide the voice. The AI just helps you get moving.

We are going to walk through the moments where AI shines in the writing process. You will see how to prompt it in ways that spark great material. You will learn how to edit what it gives you so it sounds like something only you could write. And you will get exercises that help you trust the process without handing over control.

If you have ever stared at a blank page and wished for someone to just give you a nudge, this is your chapter. You are about to learn how to turn that blank page into a playground.

Let's write something real.

Beating Writer's Block with a Robot Sidekick

Writer's block is a liar. It tells you that you have no ideas, that your words sound terrible, and that everything worth saying has already been said. It convinces you that starting is the hardest part, and finishing is even worse. And the more you listen to it, the louder it gets.

That is where AI steps in, not as a replacement, but as a disruption. It breaks the loop. It gives your brain something to react to instead of something to wrestle with.

The first time I used AI to get past a block, I was working on a short story. I had the main character and a basic plot, but no idea how to open the first scene. I stared at the screen for over an hour, rewriting the same three lines. Then, almost out of frustration, I opened ChatGPT and typed, "Write an opening paragraph for a story about a woman who wakes up in a city made entirely of glass."

What came back wasn't perfect, but it was enough. It gave me an image, a tone, and a sentence I could tweak. I copied one line, rewrote another, and used the rest as scaffolding. Within ten minutes, I was writing on my own again. The AI didn't write the story. It helped me *start* the story.

That is the trick. AI isn't meant to take over the process. It is meant to keep you moving through it. Think of it like a writing partner who never needs a coffee break and never runs out of suggestions. It will give you structure when you feel scattered, momentum when you feel slow, and surprise when your ideas feel stale.

Let's walk through a few simple ways to use AI when you feel stuck.

Start with a ridiculous prompt.
Ask the AI to write a paragraph about something absurd. For example: "Write the opening line of a novel about a time-traveling librarian who only speaks in riddles." The result might be strange or brilliant or both, but more importantly, it breaks the silence. It makes you laugh, or think, or challenge it with your own version. And just like that, the block loosens.

Try rewriting your idea through the AI's lens.

If you have a concept but no clear wording, describe it casually and ask the AI to write a short version. Something like, "Write a scene where a character realizes their dog is a secret agent, but keep it subtle." The AI will give you a draft that you can pull pieces from, reshape, or totally ignore if it sends you in a better direction.

Ask for variations.

One of my favorite tricks is asking the AI to take a line I wrote and rewrite it five different ways. I will say, "Rewrite this sentence in five tones: poetic, sarcastic, intense, mysterious, and casual." The results help me see new angles on my own writing, and they often spark better phrasing than I would have thought of on my own.

Use it to make outlines when you feel scattered.

If you have the energy to write but your brain feels foggy, try this: "Give me a four-part outline for a blog post about imposter syndrome, using a friendly and relatable tone." Once you get the outline, you can change the order, delete what you do not like, and write in your own voice. Now you are not starting from nothing. You are shaping something that already exists.

Writer's block thrives on pressure. The pressure to be original. The pressure to be polished. The pressure to impress. But AI does not care about any of that. It just gives you material. Some of it will be flat, some of it will be odd, but all of it is motion. And motion is the enemy of creative paralysis.

The more you use AI as a tool for momentum, the more confident you become in your own voice. You are not copying. You are collaborating. You are not avoiding the work. You are making the work easier to begin. So next time you feel stuck, don't wait for inspiration. Call in your sidekick. Type something weird. Ask a question. Rewrite a bad sentence. Get moving.

Your voice is still yours. The AI is just helping you clear the path.

Prompts That Hit Hard

If AI is your creative sidekick, prompts are how you talk to it. They are not just questions. They are invitations, instructions, and sparks. A weak prompt gives you generic answers. A strong one unlocks something unexpected.

The good news is, you do not need to be poetic, clever, or even particularly detailed to write a good prompt. You just need to ask the right kind of question in the right tone for what you want. That means getting specific, being curious, and sometimes embracing a little chaos.

Let's break down what makes a prompt powerful, and how you can use that power to get results that feel genuinely useful and exciting.

1. Be clear about the format you want

If you ask the AI something vague like "Tell me about creativity," you will get a Wikipedia-style overview. But if you ask, "Write a short motivational speech about how creativity helps people find their purpose," you are telling the AI what tone, format, and message you want. You are guiding it without needing to over-explain.

Try this:
"Write an opening paragraph for a novel where the main character finds a hidden letter in their grandmother's attic."
Then try changing it to:
"Write a dramatic monologue from the perspective of a teenager reading a letter they found in their grandmother's attic."

Same concept, totally different energy.

2. Use style references when needed

You can guide tone by asking for a certain style. For example:
"Write a product description for a candle that smells like regret, using the tone of a high-end perfume ad."

Or this:
"Describe a rainy city street at night in the voice of a noir detective."

These little cues help the AI know what kind of vibe you are going for. It is like telling an actor what role they are playing before they speak the line.

3. Get weird on purpose

Some of the best results come from prompts that sound like you are making them up on the spot. Why? Because AI is designed to make connections, not judgments. So when you throw it something unusual, it tries to make sense of it, and that effort often leads to something interesting.

Try this:
"Write a dialogue between a lonely vending machine and a squirrel that keeps stealing its snacks."

You might not use the result, but it gets your brain firing in a totally different way. And you can always remix the format into something more grounded later.

4. Add structure if you want usable output

If you are creating content for a project, be clear about what you need. Instead of "Help me write a blog post," say:
"Write a blog post outline about how to stay focused while working from home. Make it funny and give each section a catchy title."

Or if you are writing marketing copy:
"Create three Instagram captions for a cozy clothing brand

promoting its fall collection. Keep the tone playful and under 100 words each."

This tells the AI exactly what to build, which saves you time editing later.

5. Use prompts to rewrite or improve what you already wrote

One of the most underrated ways to use AI is as an editor. Not just for grammar, but for style and rhythm. Paste your paragraph into the chat and say:

"Can you rewrite this to feel more punchy and direct?"

Or,

"Make this paragraph more vivid, using sensory details."

Or even,

"Rewrite this sentence five different ways with different emotional tones: excited, calm, nervous, sarcastic, and hopeful."

This gives you options without making you feel stuck rewriting the same thing over and over.

6. Build prompt chains

You do not have to get everything in one go. Some of the most powerful results come from layering prompts. Start with something rough, then build on it.

Example:

Step 1: "Give me ten title ideas for a podcast about creative burnout."

Step 2: "Now write a short show description for the one titled 'The Creative Comeback.'"

Step 3: "Give me three episode titles that would fit under that show."

Step 4: "Write a teaser for episode one in a casual, witty tone."

You have just built an entire brand concept in under ten minutes.

Great prompts are less about sounding smart and more about being clear and curious. They are the bridge between your intention and the AI's output. When you ask better questions, you get better material.

Practice often. Play with tone. Push boundaries. And do not be afraid to re-prompt if the answer feels flat. You are not locked into anything. You are shaping, not settling. Prompts are not magic spells. They are tools. Learn how to swing them, and you can write just about anything.

Editing So It Still Feels Like You

Let's get something straight. Just because AI can help you write does not mean you should sound like a robot. If you are going to use it as a creative partner, your voice still needs to lead. Otherwise, it becomes content instead of communication.

The good news is that editing AI-generated writing is easier than editing your own. It gives you a draft without ego. It does not care if you rewrite everything or delete half the page. That gives you freedom. You can keep the parts that work, toss the rest, and shape the final version into something that sounds like you.

Let's talk about how to do that in a way that is fast, intentional, and actually fun.

Step one: Read it out loud

This sounds simple, but it works. When you read your writing out loud, you can instantly hear what does not sound right. You will catch awkward phrasing, weird transitions, or anything that feels too formal or too stiff.

If you read a line and think, "I would never say that," change it. Trust your instinct. AI tends to default to neutral, polished language unless you tell it otherwise. So your job is to rough it up a little. Make it messier, more human, more you.

Step two: Replace generic words with personal ones

AI loves safe words. Words like "innovative," "dynamic," "impactful," and "solutions." If it sounds like it belongs in a corporate brochure, cut it. Replace those words with something more grounded. Something visual, emotional, or specific.

For example, instead of "This project was a huge success," say, "This project actually made people stop and smile." Instead of "We faced challenges," say, "We hit a wall so hard it almost knocked the coffee out of my hand."

You do not need to be a comedian or a poet. You just need to say things the way *you* would say them.

Step three: Add rhythm and breaks

AI content can sometimes feel like a long flat road. No curves, no speed bumps, just sentence after sentence. Your job is to create a flow. That means varying sentence length. Mixing short, punchy lines with longer ones. Adding line breaks where you want the reader to pause.

If it feels like too much at once, break it up. If it feels too slow, tighten it. Writing is music. It needs rhythm.

Step four: Swap in personal references or details

This is the easiest way to make something feel like yours. Drop in your own stories, quirks, or side comments. You do not need to go full memoir, just let the reader know there is a real person behind the words.

Example:

If the AI gives you a line like, "Many people struggle with creative burnout," change it to something like, "I once spent four hours trying to write a single Instagram caption, so yeah, burnout is real."

That line suddenly feels alive. Real. Relatable.

Step five: Gut check for tone

Ask yourself, "Does this sound like me on a good day?" Not you trying to impress someone. Not you copying someone else's style. You, when you are in flow. If the writing sounds too stiff or too polished, roughen it up. If it sounds too silly and that is not your vibe, pull it back.

You are allowed to sound different in different contexts. Professional, playful, bold, weird, chill. The goal is not to find one voice forever. The goal is to make each piece of writing feel like it came from a person, not a template.

Step six: Keep the weird, if it works

Sometimes the AI will give you a phrase or a metaphor that makes no sense at first. But then you look at it again and think, "Actually, that's kind of brilliant." Keep those. Use them as inspiration. Rework them until they fit.

Do not be afraid of a little strangeness. That is where creativity lives.

Editing AI-generated content is not about cleaning it up. It is about bringing it closer to who you are. You are not just the writer anymore. You are the sculptor. The voice. The filter that turns raw material into something worth sharing.

And the more you do it, the faster it gets. You will start recognizing your voice more clearly. You will know which phrases sound right and which ones don't. You will stop asking, "Does this sound good?" and start asking, "Does this sound like me?" That is when the writing starts to click.

The AI can help you get words on the page. But only you can make them matter.

Try This Chaos

You have seen how AI can help you write faster, dodge creative blocks, and stay in your own voice. Now it is time to stretch a little. This exercise is where you go off script. You are going to try things that make no sense. On purpose.

Because sometimes creativity does not come from clarity. It comes from chaos.

This section is built to break your patterns. You are going to give the AI weird instructions, push it into unfamiliar territory, and respond to whatever it throws back. The point is not to create something perfect. The point is to loosen your grip on "getting it right."

Let's dive in.

Step one: Pick a chaotic prompt

Open your favorite AI writing tool. Then copy and paste one of these prompts, or write your own inspired by the same energy:

- Write a breakup letter from a haunted house to its former owners

- Describe a first date between a cactus and a cloud

- Tell the story of a sandwich that saves a kingdom

- Give advice from the perspective of a tired bookshelf

- Write a Yelp review of Earth by an alien tourist

These are not meant to be deep. They are designed to shake up your thinking. You will be amazed how often these odd little scenarios lead to moments of humor, insight, or strange beauty.

Step two: React and rewrite

Once the AI gives you a response, do not just read it. Interact with it. Rewrite a line in your own voice. Continue the story yourself. Flip the perspective. Turn the poem into dialogue. Pull a sentence and use it as the first line of something new. You are not grading this. You are jamming with it.

If you want, ask the AI to rewrite the same piece in a new tone. Try "gothic horror," "motivational speaker," or "ancient myth." See how it changes. You might end up loving a version you never would have thought to write.

Step three: Build on the nonsense

Pick one character, object, or phrase from the chaos you created. Use it as the seed for a new piece. Maybe the tired bookshelf becomes a narrator in a children's book. Maybe the alien tourist ends up writing tweets about Earth fashion. Follow the thread. Let it lead you somewhere.

You can also ask the AI to go deeper. For example:

- "Give me ten social media posts written by the alien tourist after visiting a mall"

- "Write a lullaby that the haunted house might whisper to itself"

- "Create a short dialogue between the cactus and a confused waiter"

Let the AI keep adding layers, and jump in whenever you feel the urge to shape or direct.

Step four: Make it yours

After a few rounds of this, you are going to have a strange collection of sentences, characters, images, or dialogue. Now take a few minutes to edit just one paragraph or idea. Bring it into your own voice. Make it sound like something you would post, publish, or send to a friend.

This is where the exercise shifts from pure play to something that could turn into a real piece of writing.

Bonus round: Share the weird

If you create something you like, post it. Screenshot it. Send it to someone who gets your humor. Start a thread or a blog or a collection of these strange collaborations. The internet loves weird energy. And your AI-fueled creativity might be more shareable than you think.

Even if you keep it private, take a moment to reflect on how fast you just created something from nothing. You did not have a plan. You did not need permission. You just showed up, typed something weird, and built from there.

That is the point.

This exercise is not about showing off. It is about proving to yourself that writing does not need to feel heavy. That momentum can start with nonsense. That your brain, when given something unexpected, will almost always find a way to respond.

And the best part? You can do this anytime. Whenever you feel stuck. Whenever you feel bored. Whenever you are tempted to scroll instead of create.

Just type something ridiculous, press go, and see what happens next.

Chapter 5: Making Art with AI

I used to think making art wasn't for me. I could barely draw a stick figure without apologizing in advance. My brain loved visuals, but my hands never got the memo. I figured that world belonged to designers, painters, and people who somehow made brush strokes look like emotions.

Then I discovered AI art tools.

At first, I treated them like a joke. I typed ridiculous prompts just to see what would happen. A flamingo riding a bike through space. A medieval knight made of pizza. A dog wearing a crown in a dystopian future. I expected glitches and garbage. Instead, I got images that made me stop scrolling and stare. That was the shift.

Suddenly, I realized I didn't need to be good with a pencil or a paintbrush. I just needed to know how to describe what I imagined. And the more I played, the more I started seeing myself as a visual creator. Not because I mastered anything, but because the barrier between my idea and the final result had disappeared.

This chapter is your invitation to do the same. You are going to learn how to use AI art tools without needing any technical skills. You will see how simple prompts can turn into bold, wild, or beautiful images. You will get practical tips, weird experiments, and creative challenges you can try with nothing more than a sentence and a screen.

You do not need to have an "eye for design." You do not need to understand color theory. All you need is the willingness to try, and a little curiosity about what might happen when you do.

If you have ever wanted to turn a daydream into a picture, this is your moment.

Let's make something visual.

My "Bad Art" Origin Story

Before I ever touched an AI art generator, I had already decided I wasn't an artist. I was the kind of person who could get stressed out by a blank sheet of printer paper. Drawing class in school? Total disaster. I once turned in a drawing of a dog that looked like a deflated squirrel. It became a running joke among my friends, and I leaned into it. I laughed about being "creatively cursed" and stuck to writing, thinking that was my lane.

Secretly though, I wanted in. I wanted to make things you could see. I loved album covers, surreal posters, strange illustrations in old storybooks. But I told myself those worlds were off limits because I didn't have the right skills. My hands didn't work like that. My mind could imagine wild things, but they never made it to the page.

That changed the day I found a text-to-image generator online.

It was late. I was messing around on the internet, looking for anything but another to-do list. I came across a tool called DALL·E Mini (now Craiyon). It asked me to type a description of anything I wanted to see. Just for fun, I wrote:

"A raccoon wearing a spacesuit, floating in front of a glowing moon, digital art style."

I hit enter and waited. About a minute later, the screen filled with images. Were they perfect? Not even close. But were they strange, vivid, and somehow exactly what I had imagined? Absolutely.

That was the first time I had ever created a visual that matched the inside of my head. I didn't draw it. I didn't paint it. But I had built it with words. And for someone who had never been able to bridge that gap between idea and image, it felt huge.

From there, I got addicted fast.

I started typing prompts every night. Giant robots in abandoned cities. Talking animals dressed like philosophers. Dreamlike forests made of glass. Sometimes the results were haunting. Sometimes hilarious. Sometimes they were just weird in a way that made me smile.

What I realized through all of it was this: creativity doesn't need to be polished. It just needs to feel like you. And these tools gave me the power to finally explore that side of myself without feeling like I was failing at something.

There was no wrong way to play. No art teacher hovering over my shoulder. No pressure to draw a perfect circle. Just a space to experiment with visuals and follow whatever idea popped into my brain.

I stopped calling myself bad at art. Not because I became good in the traditional sense, but because that label no longer applied. I was making things. Things that made me think, or laugh, or want to try again.

That is what art really is. Not a skill level, but a conversation between your imagination and the world.

If you have ever felt like visual creativity wasn't for you, I get it. If you have ever felt embarrassed by your drawings or afraid to share what you made, you are not alone. But what I found through AI is that creativity becomes easier when you take your hands out of the equation. You can build with words instead of lines. You can explore without needing to perform.

You do not need to be an artist to make art. You just need to start.

You already have ideas worth visualizing. You already know what makes you feel something. And now you have tools that can bring those ideas to life.

That is your starting line.

Free AI Art Tools I Swear By

You do not need to spend money or install anything fancy to start making amazing visuals with AI. Some of the best tools out there are free, browser-based, and surprisingly powerful. Whether you want to make art for fun, content, or side projects, these tools will get you there.

Let me walk you through the ones I keep coming back to. These are tested, beginner-friendly, and great for anyone who wants to start creating images from scratch with nothing more than an idea and a few words.

Craiyon (formerly DALL·E Mini)

Craiyon is chaotic, messy, and brilliant. It is the first AI art generator I ever tried, and it is perfect for getting weird fast. You type in a description like "a fox playing chess in a neon forest" and it gives you nine variations in about a minute.

The results are not photorealistic, but they are full of character. Sometimes the proportions are off or the faces look slightly melted, but that is part of the charm. It feels like art made during a dream. You can save the images, remix your prompt, or use them as inspiration for something else.

How to use it:

Visit www.craiyon.com, type your prompt in the box, and hit

"Draw." No account needed. You can adjust the prompt and try again as many times as you want.

Bing Image Creator

Bing's tool is powered by a version of DALL·E that gives more polished results than Craiyon. If you want clearer images, cleaner detail, and better textures, this is a solid step up. You can describe a scene in depth, and the results are often shockingly good for a free tool.

One cool feature is that you can guide the tool by using styles. You might say "a portrait of a woman made of stars, watercolor style" and get something surprisingly elegant. It also generates four image options instead of nine, but the quality tends to be much higher.

How to use it:
Go to www.bing.com/images/create. You will need to log in with a Microsoft account, but after that, it is free. You can type your prompt, choose a style if you want, and generate new images every few seconds.

Adobe Firefly (Free Tier)

If you are looking for control without needing to be a designer, Adobe Firefly is worth checking out. It lets you type in a prompt and choose the style, aspect ratio, and lighting before you generate. That makes it great for things like posters, product mockups, or anything that needs to be a little more polished.

The interface is simple and smooth. The generated images look like something you could actually use on a professional project. You also get access to text effects, like turning words into visual art made of fabric, plants, or neon signs.

How to use it:

Visit firefly.adobe.com and sign up for a free Adobe account. Then choose "Text to Image" and type your prompt. You can tweak settings for style, format, and color before clicking "Generate."

NightCafe

NightCafe offers a few different AI models to work with, which makes it great for experimentation. You can switch between styles like "artistic," "realistic," or "abstract" and see how each one interprets your idea differently.

It also has a credit system, but you get free daily credits just for logging in. If you want to create more advanced images, you can build up credits over time without ever paying. NightCafe is also one of the best platforms for browsing other people's creations and seeing what prompts they used.

How to use it:

Go to www.nightcafe.studio, sign up for a free account, and start with the "Create" button. You can select your style, input your prompt, and watch the results roll in. You can remix your images or use them as a base for something new.

Honorable Mention: Canva's Text-to-Image Tool

If you are already using Canva for design, their AI image tool is built right in. You can generate custom visuals directly in your design projects. The results are decent and integrated well with Canva's drag-and-drop layout, which makes it a great option if you want to use your images for social posts, covers, or websites.

These tools are not just fun to play with. They give you actual creative power. You can make something that did not exist an hour ago. You can visualize characters, design a brand mood board, or turn strange thoughts into surreal digital posters.

And all you need is a sentence.

The trick is not to overthink it. You do not need to know what the final image should look like. Just describe what is in your head and let the AI surprise you. Sometimes the best part is seeing what it thinks you meant. You can go weird, go pretty, go serious, or go chaotic. You can use these images for inspiration or put them straight into your projects. You are the creator now.

No software. No drawing skills. Just you and your ideas, visualized.

Stealing Picasso's Vibe

One of the coolest things about AI art is its ability to mimic different styles. You can type in a simple description like "a cat playing piano" and instantly get versions that look abstract, hyper-realistic, vintage, dreamy, or cartoonish. The AI does not just understand what you want. It knows how to dress it up in the style of your choice.

This is where things start to feel like magic.

The first time I realized this, I was playing around with a prompt in Bing Image Creator. I typed, "a ballerina made of smoke, digital painting." It looked nice. Soft edges, a little dramatic. Then I changed the prompt slightly and added "in the style of Picasso." The results were wild. Angular limbs, bold colors, fractured space. Suddenly, it felt like I had stumbled into a surreal gallery.

I tried it again, this time with "a robot drinking tea in the style of van Gogh." The textures popped. The colors swirled. The background looked like it had been painted in a hurry but with purpose. I had no idea AI could understand nuance like that. But it did. And it opened a creative door I didn't know I had access to.

You can do this too. You can take your simple ideas and filter them through the lens of legendary artists, graphic design eras, or modern trends. You are not just generating pictures anymore. You are remixing art history into something new.

Here's how to get started.

Pick a subject that feels playful or personal

It can be anything. A scene, an object, an emotion. Try things like:

- "A lonely astronaut walking through a desert"

- "A tree made of music notes"

- "A wolf howling into a canyon of mirrors"

These give you something visual, but with room for interpretation.

Add a style reference

Now add to your prompt with a phrase like:

- "in the style of Monet"

- "digital painting, 80s synthwave style"

- "art nouveau poster design"

- "as a woodblock print"

- "flat illustration, modern branding aesthetic"

This tells the AI how to frame your idea. If you are not sure what to reference, just explore. Type in different styles and see how it changes the result.

Try mixing styles together

This is where things get interesting. You can layer two or more styles to create something unique.

Try:

"A fox in a trench coat walking through a rainy city, in the style of Studio Ghibli meets noir comic book."

Or:

"A goddess of time made from gears and vines, part steampunk, part classical sculpture."

You are not just copying styles. You are blending them to create your own visual language.

Use this as a way to find your own taste

Over time, you will notice what you are drawn to. Maybe you like pastel textures. Maybe you love harsh shadows and neon edges. Maybe you keep coming back to that stained-glass look. The more prompts you write, the more you start defining what *your* vibe is.

That's the part Picasso would approve of. You are not just borrowing. You are transforming.

Tips for better results

- Include colors. Words like "muted tones," "high contrast," or "warm lighting" help guide the vibe.

- Include medium. Add things like "digital painting," "oil on canvas," or "ink sketch" to shape the texture.

- Mention mood. Words like "dreamy," "melancholy," or "playful" will steer the emotional tone.

Here's a full sample prompt to try:

"A vintage typewriter floating underwater, surrounded by jellyfish, dreamy lighting, in the style of surrealist collage art."

When you generate images like this, you are doing more than making art. You are training your eye. You are learning how different influences shape the final piece. You are becoming a creative director of your own visual experiments.

You do not need to be an expert on art history. You do not need to know the difference between cubism and expressionism. You just need to pay attention to what makes your brain light up. If something feels exciting, run with it. Tweak it. Change the color palette. Add a new twist. Each image is just one version of an idea. You can keep evolving it until it feels like yours.

And that is the key. You are not stealing Picasso's vibe. You are borrowing it for a moment, adding your own voice, and creating something that never existed before.

Make This: Your First AI Art Challenge

You've seen what's possible. You know the tools. You've played with styles and pushed your imagination into visual form. Now it's your turn to create something from scratch.

This is your first official AI art challenge. It's not about being perfect. It's about seeing how far you can go with a few prompts, a little curiosity, and a few rounds of remixing. This is where you start building your own creative momentum.

Here's how the challenge works. You'll follow a four-step process:

1. Generate an image.

2. Remix it with a twist.

3. Build a story around it.

4. Share or save it.

Let's walk through each step together.

Step one: Generate your first image

Pick one of the following prompts, or write your own using the same format. Keep it short, visual, and a little strange.

- "A sleeping giant curled around a lighthouse, pastel color palette"

- "A child discovering a floating library in the sky, watercolor style"

- "A deer with galaxies in its antlers, dramatic lighting, surrealist painting"

Open any of the tools we've covered (Craiyon, Bing Image Creator, Adobe Firefly, NightCafe), copy in the prompt, and hit generate.

Pick the image that stands out most to you. It does not need to be perfect. It just needs to feel interesting.

Step two: Remix the image with a twist

Take that original idea and change it. Not a lot. Just enough to shift the mood, setting, or style.

Use one of these methods:

- Shift the art style. If your first image was a painting, try a flat graphic look next.

- Change the time of day or season. If your scene was at night, try it in morning light or during a snowstorm.

- Zoom in on a single detail. If your original image showed a landscape, ask the AI to focus on a close-up of one object in the scene.

Here's an example:

Original prompt:
"A fox sitting under a glowing mushroom, fantasy style"

Remix:
"Close-up of the mushroom's surface, with tiny glowing insects crawling across, digital art"

Generate again. Compare. Do you like the shift? Is there more to explore? Keep going until something clicks.

Step three: Build a micro-story

Now that you've got one or two images you like, write a short story, poem, or character sketch inspired by what you see.

Use these questions to get started:

- Who lives in this scene?

- What is happening just before or just after this moment?

- What emotion does the image hold, and why?

- If this were a dream, what would it mean?

Write one paragraph. That's enough. It doesn't have to explain everything. It just needs to take the image one step further and turn it into a moment that feels alive.

Step four: Save it or share it

Download your image. Pair it with your story or caption. Post it somewhere, save it in a folder, or send it to a friend. Don't overthink it. This is just the beginning.

If you feel like it, give the piece a title. Treat it like something that deserves attention, even if it only took you ten minutes. That is the point. You just made something that didn't exist before.

Here's a bonus round if you're feeling bold:
Create three images from the same original prompt, each in a different style. For example, a realistic version, a cartoon version, and a vintage poster version. Then compare them. Which one feels most "you"? Which one tells the best story? Which one surprises you?

This is how you start building a creative style. Not by picking one tool and sticking with it, but by trying everything and seeing what lights you up. Remember, your first AI art challenge is not about showing off. It's about showing up. The tools are here. Your imagination is ready. All you have to do is start.

You're officially creating visuals now. Not someday. Not when you get better. Right now.

Chapter 6: AI Music Experiments from My Bedroom Studio

Music was always something I admired from a distance. I loved it, studied it, obsessed over lyrics and playlists, but never actually made any myself. I didn't know how to play instruments. I couldn't read sheet music. The idea of composing something felt impossible, like trying to paint with invisible ink.

That changed the day I made a song with AI.

No fancy equipment. No software downloads. Just a simple website that asked what kind of mood I wanted, what genre I liked, and what kind of instruments to include. A few clicks later, I had a track playing through my headphones that I had helped create. It was not a chart-topper, but it was mine. And it made something click.

Music was no longer locked behind talent. It was open to curiosity.

This chapter is for anyone who has ever dreamed of making music but thought they were not musical enough. You will learn how to use free AI tools to create custom soundtracks, loops, ambient vibes, and full songs with zero technical knowledge. We are going to explore how sound works as creative expression, how you can guide the mood and tone of your tracks, and how these tools can help you make music even if you cannot sing a note.

Whether you want to score a short film, make background music for your writing sessions, or just vibe out and experiment, there is something here for you. You do not need a home studio. You do not even need headphones. Just a browser and a few ideas.

We are going to walk through the tools I use, the sounds I've made, and the weird little discoveries that turned my laptop into a beat lab.

Let's plug in.

The Day I Made a Song in My Pajamas

It started as a joke. I was sitting on my bed in pajamas, procrastinating a writing deadline, and I typed "free AI music generator" into a search bar. I had zero expectations. I figured it would be like those old ringtone websites where every track sounded like a rejected video game loop.

Instead, I landed on a site called Soundraw. It asked me to choose a genre. I picked "lofi" because I wanted something chill. Then it gave me a list of moods. I picked "dreamy." That alone felt weirdly empowering, like ordering a custom emotion from a menu.

I clicked generate.

Thirty seconds later, a song started playing. It was smooth and echoey, with layered synths and gentle percussion. Not amazing, but shockingly decent. I hit play again. This time, I listened closer. The tempo felt right. The structure had dynamics. The whole thing sounded like it belonged in the background of a short film or a study playlist.

And I made it. In my pajamas. With zero knowledge of music theory.

That was the moment something shifted. I realized that AI music generators were not toys. They were actual tools. They gave people like me a way into a space we had always loved but never felt welcome in.

I spent the rest of that afternoon clicking through different genres. I made a moody ambient track that felt like walking through fog. I made an upbeat synth loop that would have fit perfectly in an indie video game. I even made something that sounded suspiciously like the intro music to a true crime podcast.

All of it came from choosing a few simple settings and letting the AI build the base. Once I had the core track, I could tweak the structure. I could cut out parts, repeat sections, or change the mood. I was not composing from scratch. I was shaping sound that already existed.

It felt like being a music director instead of a musician.

That night, I exported my favorite track and played it in the background while I cooked dinner. It was not about showing off. It was about the feeling. That quiet sense of pride when you make something, even something small, that didn't exist an hour ago.

Since then, I have used AI tools to make music for writing sessions, background tracks for short videos, and even sound experiments I never shared with anyone. I have made things that are calm, weird, cinematic, glitchy, and nostalgic. And every time I click generate, I get that same rush of surprise.

It still amazes me that I can make music with no gear, no training, and no stress. All I need is a vibe and a few clicks. So if you have ever looked at music like a locked room you do not have the key for, I am here to tell you the door is wide open. You do not have to know chords. You do not have to write lyrics. You do not need a microphone or a beat pad or a subscription to a fancy software suite.

You can make a song in your pajamas. And you might even like it.

Free Sound Tools That Make You Feel Like a Producer

You do not need a music studio to sound like you have one. Today's AI music tools are so good, they make you feel like a low-key producer in your living room. No cables, no keyboards, no need to understand what a compressor does. You just set the mood, press a few buttons, and boom. You have a track.

Here are the free tools I keep coming back to, each one beginner-friendly but surprisingly flexible. If you have ever wanted to make your own soundtrack, background music, or something just for fun, these are the ones to start with.

Soundraw

Soundraw was my first AI music crush. The site is fast, clean, and lets you pick the vibe right from the jump. You choose your genre, then select the mood and energy level. Once you hit generate, it gives you a playlist of tracks that match your settings.

Here is what makes it awesome. Every track is customizable. You can open one up and change its length, loop certain parts, mute instruments, or adjust how intense the music feels. It is like sculpting a song instead of writing it.

Try this:

Go to soundraw.io and click "Create Music." Pick "Lofi" or "Cinematic" as your genre. Set the mood to something like "Peaceful" or "Epic." Generate a few tracks and listen. Pick one you like, then use the timeline editor to mute an instrument or change the chorus section. Download the final version and use it as background music while you work.

Boomy

Boomy is great for people who want a faster, more playful experience. You pick a style, click "Create Song," and get a full track in about thirty seconds. From there, you can fine-tune the arrangement or just roll with what you get.

Boomy also lets you add vocals with simple text input, though that part takes a little experimentation to sound good. If you are interested in creating short songs, theme music, or loops for content, this is an easy and fun option.

Try this:

Go to boomy.com and sign up for a free account. Click "Create" and choose a genre like "Relaxing" or "Ambient." Generate a few songs, then save the ones you like. Use them for meditation, journaling, or just to set a tone for the day.

Melobytes

Melobytes is pure chaos in the best way. You can turn images into music, text into soundscapes, or even upload your own audio and have it remixed into something wild. It is not for polished production, but it is fantastic for experimentation.

Try this:

Visit melobytes.com and choose "Text to Song." Type a sentence like "I dreamed of a robot singing lullabies in the rain." Choose a language, a genre, and a vocal style, then hit generate. It will spit out a bizarre little music video that feels part art project, part fever dream.

Beatoven.ai

Beatoven is designed more for content creators and filmmakers who need music for specific moods and scenes. You choose a theme like "uplifting" or "tense," set a duration, and get a track built for your exact use case.

You can also break the song into sections, change moods midway, and download royalty-free music that is ready to use anywhere. It feels more structured than Boomy or Melobytes, which makes it great for professional-looking projects.

Try this:

Head to beatoven.ai and try the "Create a track" button. Choose a project type, set the mood, and generate a short clip. Use it as background music in a video or combine it with images you generated in earlier chapters.

All of these tools work in the browser, and most do not require any musical knowledge. You do not have to know what a bridge or a chorus is. You just have to be curious and willing to listen to what happens when you click.

You will find that each platform has its own personality. Some are sleek and cinematic. Others are strange and glitchy. The more you explore, the more you will figure out what sounds like you.

If you want to level up, try combining them. Use Soundraw to make a base track, then bring it into a free audio editor like Audacity and layer it with vocals or sound effects. Or create a Boomy song and use it as the score for a video with AI-generated visuals.

You do not need to do everything at once. Just make one thing. Play one track. Download one loop that makes your brain light up. That is the start. Because once you feel what it is like to create music with no pressure, no gatekeeping, and no rules, you will want to keep going.

Mixing It Up Like a Bedroom DJ

The first time I made a track with AI, I liked it. But the second time I took that track, chopped it up, and layered a few extra sounds on top, I loved it. That was the moment it stopped feeling like something the AI made and started feeling like something *I* made.

This is the difference between generating music and mixing it. Generating is fun. Mixing makes it personal.

You do not need to be a DJ or know how to produce music. You just need to learn how to stack, shape, and tweak what the AI gives you. It is like decorating a cake that's already baked. The base is there, but you decide what flavors, textures, or weird toppings to add.

Here's how to start mixing your own AI-created tracks from the comfort of your bedroom.

Step one: Pick your base track

Start with something you already generated from Soundraw, Boomy, or Beatoven. Choose a track that has a strong rhythm or mood, even if it is a little too simple. That simplicity gives you room to build on it.

Download the file and import it into a free audio editor like Audacity or BandLab. These programs look a little intimidating at first, but all you really need is the ability to drag and drop, split a track, and adjust the volume of different layers.

Step two: Add another layer

Now think about what you want to add. Do you want vocals? Try recording yourself or generating voice clips with AI voice tools. Do you want atmosphere? Add rain sounds, crowd noise, or city ambience. You can find free sound libraries at sites like Freesound.org or Mixkit.

Drag those audio clips into your project and place them alongside or on top of your base track. Line up the timing so it flows naturally. Adjust the volume so nothing is overpowering the rest. Trust your ear.

This is your first real mix.

Step three: Create contrast
One trick that gives your music dimension is contrast. If the whole song feels the same from start to finish, it will start to blend into the background. Try doing one of the following:

- Cut the drums for a few seconds in the middle of the track

- Add a soft sound effect that builds up just before the final chorus

- Lower the volume in one section and raise it gradually, like a slow wave coming in

These little changes make your song feel like it has movement and energy. They give it a story.

Step four: Try looping or sampling yourself
Here's where things get fun. Pick one line or beat from the track you made and copy it. Paste it multiple times to create a repeating rhythm. Now add a second loop on top of it. This is how a lot of music is built. Layer by layer. Loop by loop.

You can even sample yourself. Record a simple vocal or hum a short melody. Then drag that audio into your mix. Stretch it.

Reverse it. Filter it until it sounds completely different. Suddenly, your own voice becomes an instrument.

Step five: Give it a name and bounce it out
Once you have a track that feels good, name it. Export it as an MP3 or WAV file. Save it somewhere you can find again. You just made a song from scratch. You are now officially your own music project.

You can keep it to yourself or use it as background for your writing, videos, or daydreaming sessions. If you are feeling bold, upload it to SoundCloud or share it with a friend. The point is not to impress anyone. The point is to start building a sound that feels like yours.

Mixing is not about mastering audio. It is about shaping feeling. You are creating something that makes your space feel a certain way. You are setting a tone, telling a story, or just vibing out with the weird little sounds in your head.

And once you start, you will never hear music the same way again. You will notice layers. You will listen more closely. You will understand how songs are not magic, they are just choices.

Choices you are now able to make.

Try This: Build a Track from Vibe to Finish

This is your chance to put it all together. You have played with the tools, generated a few tracks, maybe even remixed something. Now it is time to go from idea to finished piece. This is your challenge: build a full track from start to finish using free tools and nothing but your imagination.

You do not need to make a masterpiece. The goal is to create a mood. A vibe. A piece of sound that feels like something you would use, share, or just keep as proof that yes, you made music.

Here's your step-by-step guide. No pressure. Just flow.

Step one: Choose your vibe
Close your eyes for a second and picture a scene. Not a song, a scene. Maybe it is a rainy street at midnight. A spaceship docking on a glowing planet. A walk through the woods with your headphones in. Choose one that gives you a feeling.

Now write a one-sentence description of it. That is your creative compass for this challenge.

Examples:

- A quiet moment in a coffee shop while the world rushes past outside

- A forgotten city where plants have taken over everything

- A dream where you are floating through time, not quite awake, not quite asleep

Step two: Generate your base track

Head to Soundraw, Boomy, or Beatoven. Pick a genre that fits the vibe you just imagined. Set the mood. Select your energy level. Then hit generate and listen to the options. Pick the one that gets closest to the feeling you are going for. If none are quite right, tweak the settings and try again. You are looking for something that could be the soundtrack to your scene.

Download the track once it feels right.

Step three: Layer in texture

Open your track in an audio editor like Audacity or BandLab. This is where you start shaping it. Add a second layer that enhances the mood. It could be:

- Ambient noise (wind, birds, street sounds, static)

- A single piano note that repeats softly

- Your voice, whispered or altered

- A sound effect from a free site like Freesound.org

Line it up with your original track. Adjust the volume so it blends. Do not overthink it. Just follow your ear.

Step four: Structure it with intention

Even short tracks benefit from a little structure. Think of it like a journey. Where does the energy rise? Where does it fall? What happens at the start, the middle, the end?

Try one of these basic templates:

- **Intro > Build > Drop > Outro**

- **Calm > Rise > Calm again**

- **Loop > Surprise moment > Loop again**

Use your editor to split and move sections around. You might mute the beat in one spot, or repeat a certain part twice to give it weight. These little changes turn your track into a full experience.

Step five: Title it and export

Give your track a name that fits the mood. It does not have to be clever. Just something that matches the vibe you imagined at the start. Export it as an MP3 or WAV. Play it back and listen all the way through.

Congratulations. You just built a track from nothing but a vibe.

Bonus challenge: Pair it with visuals

Want to go even further? Use a tool like Craiyon or Bing Image Creator to generate artwork that fits your track. Type a version of your original scene prompt into the image tool and save the results. Use that as your album art or background if you ever share the track.

Now you have a complete micro project. A visual and a sound, both created by you, guided by AI, and built from your imagination.

This exercise is not about technical perfection. It is about creative ownership. You are the one choosing the vibe. You are the one shaping the sound. You are the one who gets to say, "This is mine."

And whether you make lo-fi beats, cinematic scores, ambient soundscapes, or something totally experimental, the tools are here to help you keep creating. So hit save. Hit play. And know that your music journey just started.

Chapter 7: Brainstorming Like a Maniac with AI

There is a specific kind of creative energy that shows up when you are on a roll. The ideas keep coming. You are scribbling notes, making voice memos, sending texts to yourself. You feel unstoppable. It is rare, it is messy, and it is addictive.

This chapter is about how to trigger that kind of energy on demand, using AI as your brainstorming partner.

AI is perfect for this. It does not slow down. It does not second-guess. It does not worry about whether an idea is weird or useful. It just keeps throwing options at you, and that is exactly what you need in a good storming session. Volume over perfection. Chaos before clarity.

Whether you are planning a creative project, starting a business, writing a story, building a brand, or just trying to come up with your next big move, this chapter is your jam. You are going to learn how to prompt AI to generate dozens of ideas in a few minutes. You will learn how to sort through the mess and find the gold. You will learn how to keep your brain in motion even when you are tired, blocked, or bored.

And just like with music and art, the secret is not making the perfect choice right away. The secret is momentum. More ideas lead to better ideas. Even the weird ones matter. Especially the weird ones.

Get ready to turn on the faucet and let the ideas pour out.

This is brainstorming, upgraded.

Idea Avalanche: Why Quantity Beats Quality at First

When you are brainstorming, your first instinct might be to wait for the perfect idea. The one that feels shiny, brilliant, and fully formed. But here is the truth no one really says out loud: most great ideas are buried under piles of weird, obvious, and terrible ones.

That is not a flaw in the process. That *is* the process.

Quantity leads to quality. That is not just motivational fluff, it is backed by how creativity actually works. The more ideas you generate, the more chances you have to stumble into something original. The trick is not trying to get it right on the first shot. The trick is getting as many shots as possible.

This is where AI becomes your secret weapon.

Normally, coming up with ten ideas takes time. Your brain slows down after three or four. You start second-guessing. You ask,

"Has this been done before?" or "Is this even good?" But AI does not care. It will give you twenty, fifty, even a hundred variations in a few seconds. Most will be average. Some will be bad. And a few will be gold. Let me show you how that works in practice.

Let's say you are trying to come up with a product idea. Something simple, just to practice. You open ChatGPT and type:

"Give me ten creative product ideas for people who work from home."

Here are some responses you might get:

1. A desk mat that doubles as a whiteboard

2. A mug that tracks caffeine intake

3. A plant pot that reacts to Zoom meetings

4. A wearable blanket with built-in Bluetooth

5. A digital window that shows changing scenery

6. A scented diffuser that releases focus-enhancing aromas

7. A chair that gently reminds you to stretch

8. A pen that transcribes your handwriting

9. A coaster that tracks how often you hydrate

10. A wall clock that suggests break times

Now you have ten different starting points. Maybe none of them are perfect. But a few probably make you smile or think, *That could work if I tweak it.* You take number five and imagine it as a customizable background for people without windows in their home office. You combine it with number six and suddenly you are thinking about multisensory setups that change throughout the day. You are no longer stuck. You are building.

That is the idea avalanche. Start with volume. Let the momentum carry you. The more ideas you generate, the less pressure you feel. You are not committing to anything yet. You are just making the pile bigger so you can dig through it later.

This method works for everything. Need story ideas? Ask for twenty opening lines. Starting a podcast? Ask for fifteen episode topics. Building a course? Ask for a list of possible modules. You can even ask the AI to give you ideas grouped by theme or difficulty.

Want to level it up? Try this:

"Give me twenty creative business names for a cozy candle brand, sorted by tone: playful, elegant, edgy."

You will get lists that spark different parts of your brain. Some will make you laugh. Some will feel off. Some will surprise you. But now you have something to work with. You are reacting, not inventing from thin air.

Once the ideas are flowing, your job is to shape them. Cross out the boring ones. Star the interesting ones. Combine two that do not belong together and see what happens. Ask follow-up prompts like:

- "Give me ten taglines for this idea"

- "Write a short pitch explaining how it works"

- "What kind of person would love this?"

- "What could I call the premium version?"

Every prompt gives you a new pile to sift through. You are building an avalanche on purpose, knowing that somewhere inside it is your breakthrough.

The biggest creative block is not lack of talent. It is fear of bad ideas. AI removes that fear. It gives you the freedom to explore without wasting time or feeling stuck. You do not have to be brilliant. You just have to be open to the flow.

So next time you sit down to brainstorm, skip the pressure. Go for quantity. Go fast. Go weird. Let the avalanche hit. You can clean it up later. Right now, you just need to start the storm.

Prompts That Punch Above Their Weight

Some prompts are just built different. You type them in and suddenly your screen fills with gold. They do not waste time. They skip the fluff. They give you ideas that make your brain sit up straight.

In this section, we are going to look at those kinds of prompts. These are the ones I go to when I need ideas fast. They work because they are focused, specific, and flexible. You can use them for content, side hustles, personal projects, or just when you feel stuck and want something to react to.

Let's start with a few foundational templates and build from there.

1. "Give me 10 ideas for [project] that feel [tone or vibe]."
This one is simple but powerful. You are giving the AI a clear target (what you want ideas for) and a mood or style to shape the results.

Examples:

- "Give me 10 ideas for a podcast about creativity that feel playful and unexpected."

- "Give me 10 ideas for a YouTube channel about productivity that feel calming and honest."

- "Give me 10 gift product ideas for people who love coffee that feel luxurious but quirky."

You can replace the tone with anything. Use words like bold, soft, edgy, relaxing, hilarious, poetic, futuristic, nostalgic. This one tweak changes everything.

2. "List 20 problems faced by [specific group], then turn each one into a creative product or solution."

This one is great for invention-style thinking. You start with empathy. You end with innovation.

Examples:

- "List 20 daily problems faced by remote workers, then turn each one into a fun and useful product."

- "List 20 annoying things about living in a small apartment, then brainstorm solutions."

- "List 20 struggles of beginner writers, then give me tools or services that could help."

You are not just getting random ideas. You are getting purpose-driven ideas.

3. "Give me 15 odd mashups of [thing] and [thing] that could turn into interesting projects."

Mashups unlock novelty. They force the brain to connect ideas it would not normally combine.

Examples:

- "Give me 15 odd mashups of meditation and gaming."

- "Give me 15 mashups of cooking and time travel."

- "Give me 15 mashups of journaling and outer space."

What you get back might be ridiculous, but inside the chaos there is always at least one spark worth chasing.

4. "List 10 themes or metaphors I could use to explore [topic]."
Themes and metaphors help make ideas feel deeper, richer, and more human.

Examples:

- "List 10 themes I could use to write about burnout without saying the word burnout."

- "List 10 metaphors to explore the feeling of starting over in life."

- "List 10 ways to describe anxiety using natural imagery or weather patterns."

You are not just collecting ideas. You are collecting language that gives your ideas more emotional weight.

5. "If [famous creator or brand] had to make something in [new space], what would it look like?"

This is the prompt for creative mimicry. It pulls style and identity into new contexts.

Examples:

- "If Pixar made a cooking show, what would it be called? What would the vibe be?"

- "If Marie Kondo launched a fashion line, what would the key pieces be?"

- "If Banksy designed a wellness app, what would it do?"

This is especially fun for brand builders and content creators who want to explore style and voice.

Bonus Round: The Wild Card Stack

If you want something completely chaotic and fun, try stacking concepts into a single prompt.

Example:

"Give me 10 startup ideas that blend artificial intelligence, plants, and nostalgia. Make half of them sound completely impractical but still lovable."

You will get everything from AI-powered bonsai trees to houseplants that sing 90s R&B when watered. And somewhere in that madness, something real will click.

The magic of these prompts is not just in the output. It is in the way they shift your mindset. They give you permission to try ideas you might never have thought of on your own. They help you step outside your usual creative lane and explore new ones without judgment.

You are not trying to get everything perfect. You are trying to get something started.

So the next time you are staring at a blank doc or a foggy brain, come back to one of these. Drop it into your favorite AI tool. Skim what comes back. Copy the one that hits. Then keep building.

These are your creative launch buttons. Press one.

Picking Winners from the Mess

Once the ideas start pouring in, you hit a new kind of challenge. It is not about coming up with ideas anymore. It is about figuring out what to do with the giant pile sitting in front of you.

This part can feel overwhelming if you are not ready for it. You scroll through twenty, maybe fifty AI-generated ideas. Some are wild. Some are boring. Some are kind of brilliant but also kind of confusing. The trick is knowing how to sort through it without overthinking or losing momentum.

Here is a process that works.

Step one: Gut check the whole list

Before you start ranking or judging anything, read the full list. Out loud if possible. Notice what makes you smile. Notice what makes you pause. Sometimes an idea will hit you in a quiet way. Other times, something silly will catch you off guard and make you want to run with it. That is what you are looking for. Not logic. Not marketability. Just raw reaction.

Mark anything that sparks interest, even if you are not sure why yet.

Step two: Look for patterns

Now that you have skimmed everything, start grouping the ideas. Some might naturally cluster together around a theme or tone. Others might feel like variations of the same concept. Grouping helps you see where your thinking is going. It also helps you realize when five okay ideas might actually be one great one if combined.

For example, if you asked for podcast episode ideas and got:

- "The day I almost quit my side hustle"

- "How to bounce back from burnout"

- "Why taking a break saved my business"

You can see the pattern: resilience. Instead of picking just one, maybe your best move is to combine them into a mini-series or build a larger framework around that theme.

Step three: Eliminate the obvious or boring

Cut anything that feels too generic or safe. These are often ideas that do not bring anything new to the table. They are fine. They are just not *yours*. If you have seen the concept five times before, and it does not excite you to do your own take, toss it. You are not trying to keep everything. You are trying to find what feels alive.

Step four: Stress test your top three

Take your top three picks and start asking better questions. Push each idea a little to see what it is made of.

- Can you picture this idea being shared?

- Can you imagine working on it for more than a day?

- Could it lead to more ideas later?

- What kind of person would get excited about this?

You do not need full answers. You are just looking for depth. If an idea holds up under a little pressure, that is a good sign. If it falls apart or loses steam fast, it might not be worth pursuing.

Step five: Prompt deeper

Take your winning idea and go back to the AI for a second round.
Ask questions like:

- "Write a short pitch for this idea"

- "What is a creative way to explain this to a friend?"

- "What is the opposite version of this concept?"

- "How could I turn this into a product, a story, or a challenge?"

You are not polishing yet. You are just exploring how flexible
the idea is. Good ideas grow when you press on them. Great ones
start to unfold new directions.

Step six: Pick and commit (lightly)

Now choose the one that feels best and commit to it. Not forever.
Just enough to explore it further. Give yourself permission to run
with it for an hour or a day without judging. Make a sketch. Write
a page. Build a draft. Whatever your thing is, do it.

And remember: you can always pivot. The real win is forward
motion.

You are not here to be a perfect filter. You are here to be a
curious editor. Your job is not to know everything right away. It is
to notice what has potential, press on it, and see what shakes loose.

AI can generate endless ideas. But only you can choose the ones worth chasing.

That choice is where your creativity shows up.

Try This: Brainstorming Workout

This is not your typical journaling session. This is a rapid-fire idea workout built to stretch your creative brain, shake loose the stuck parts, and show you how fast you can go when you stop chasing perfection. This is the part where you do, not think.

Set aside 25 minutes. Open your AI tool of choice, a blank doc, or even a notebook. You are going to run through a four-part creative circuit. No pressure, no polishing, just pure motion.

Let's go.

Round 1: Idea Blitz (7 minutes)

Pick a theme or a general area you care about. It could be broad, like "self-improvement," "travel," "relationships," or "weird inventions." Now, ask your AI tool this:

"Give me 25 creative ideas related to [your topic], sorted into fun or surprising categories."

Example prompt:

"Give me 25 unique ideas for a newsletter about creative confidence. Group them into playful, bold, reflective, and weird."

Once the list appears, copy it into your doc. Skim it fast. Highlight anything that feels interesting, confusing, or exciting.

Round 2: Follow the Spark (5 minutes)

Pick one idea from the list that gave you a reaction. It does not need to be your favorite. Just something that made you pause. Ask the AI a follow-up:

"Write a one-paragraph pitch for this idea."

Then ask:

"How could I turn this into a product, a piece of content, or a short story?"

Write down any pieces that stand out. Do not edit. Do not second-guess. Just follow the thread.

Round 3: Flip and Remix (5 minutes)

Take that idea and flip it on its head. Ask the AI to help:

"What is the opposite of this idea?"

"How would this idea look in a totally different industry or medium?"

"Turn this idea into a challenge, a game, or a physical experience."

Now you have the same seed, but planted in different soil. Pick the remix that feels most fun. You are not picking the best. You are picking what feels alive.

Round 4: Make a Mini Pitch (8 minutes)

Now it is time to bring it home. Take the version of the idea you like most and turn it into a tiny pitch. Use this structure:

- Title

- Short description (2 sentences)

- Who it's for

- Why it matters

- What the next step could be

Here is a quick example:

Title: Inbox Adventures

Description: A weekly newsletter where your inbox turns into a choose-your-own-adventure game. Every edition ends with a reader vote that changes the next chapter.

Who it's for: People who love storytelling, surprises, and interactive fiction

Why it matters: It makes newsletters fun again and builds a tight reader community

Next step: Write the first email episode

Now you have a creative concept that came from nothing but a theme and a willingness to move fast.

You can run this workout as often as you want. Change the topic. Change the prompts. Use it for writing, product ideas, brand building, or pure creative play. The point is not the final product. The point is to train your brain to stay loose, flexible, and curious.

The more you do this, the easier it gets. You stop treating ideas like rare gems and start seeing them as abundant, like pebbles on the shore. The good ones will stick. The rest will roll away. Your creative muscles get stronger every time you show up like this. This is how you train to think like a maker. Like a problem solver. Like someone who does not wait for permission to create.

And all it takes is a timer, a prompt, and a little chaos.

Chapter 8: Side Hustles and Cash Experiments with AI

You've generated ideas. You've made visuals, written stories, built soundtracks, and probably surprised yourself a few times along the way. Now it's time to ask a different kind of question. What happens when you put that creativity to work?

This chapter is where we shift into hustle mode. Not in a cold, startup-grind kind of way. More like testing your ideas in the real world to see what sticks, what earns, and what feels fun enough to keep doing. It is about using AI to build tiny businesses, launch playful experiments, and create digital products without needing a team, a budget, or a business degree.

The line between a fun project and a real income stream is thinner than most people think. You do not need a massive following. You do not need investors. You just need something people want, a way to talk about it, and a system to deliver it. AI makes all three of those pieces easier than ever.

You are going to learn how to use AI to brainstorm product ideas, test offers, build assets, write listings, and even automate parts of your workflow. Whether you want to run a weekend side hustle, create a mini shop, launch a newsletter, or just experiment for fun, this chapter gives you a playbook.

The goal is not to promise overnight success. The goal is to give you tools that let you try, learn, and build as you go. You will see how creative income does not have to look traditional. Sometimes your weirdest idea is your most valuable one. Sometimes a small win turns into something much bigger.

This is about turning creativity into momentum. And momentum into something that earns.

Let's build something real.

Cash from Chaos

Making money from your creativity used to feel like a distant dream. It was something people did after years of training, building, posting, failing, and repeating. But now, with AI tools in your back pocket, the distance between a fun idea and a functioning income stream is shorter than ever. You do not need to quit your job, brand yourself as an entrepreneur, or spend six months building a perfect product. You just need to be willing to test something small, right now.

The chaos part is important. Because real-world experiments are messy. You are going to try things that flop. You are going to write listings that no one clicks. You are going to make digital products that three people download. That is normal. That is part of the process. But inside that mess, you will also discover what works. And you might even stumble into something that not only makes money but feels like it belongs to you in a way nothing else has.

When I first started playing with AI-powered projects, I didn't have a plan. I was messing around with a writing prompt generator I built using ChatGPT and some copy-paste logic. I packaged it as a free download on Gumroad just to see what would happen. I gave it a silly name, wrote a quick description, and posted it on Twitter. Within a week, I had fifty downloads. Two people sent me thank you messages. One person asked if I offered a paid version with more categories.

So I made one.

It took me a single afternoon to build out extra prompt packs, add a few design elements with Canva, and write a more polished landing page with AI help. I priced it at ten dollars. People bought it. Not in huge numbers. But enough that it felt real. Enough to pay for lunch and spark new ideas.

The whole thing came from chaos. I wasn't trying to build a business. I was testing an idea to see what happened. I used free tools, fast writing, and a healthy sense of "Why not?" That mindset is exactly what this chapter is about.

If you are reading this thinking, I don't have anything to sell, remember this: products do not have to be complex. They do not have to be physical. They do not even have to be totally original. They just need to solve a small problem, entertain someone, teach something, or make a task easier.

You can create digital journals, printable planners, aesthetic backgrounds, curated lists, writing tools, AI prompt packs, voiceovers, story outlines, character designs, niche guides, or starter kits. You can bundle up useful things you've already made and turn them into value for someone else. If you have made it, you can probably sell it. If you can describe it, you can build it with AI.

The mindset here is not build and hope. It is test and learn.

Start small. Pick one idea. Use AI to help you build the pieces. A product description. A name. A cover image. A sample post or walkthrough. Get it out there in front of people, even if that means one post on social media or a quiet listing on a marketplace. Then watch what happens. What do people respond to? What do they ignore? What could you make next, now that you've learned something?

You are not chasing a big break. You are building creative proof. Every tiny product or offer you put out is a signal. Every small sale is validation. Every quiet failure is direction.

This is what it looks like to make cash from chaos.

You are not just monetizing. You are exploring. You are shaping ideas into something real. You are learning how your creativity fits into the world and how it can support you in ways you did not expect. You are not waiting to be ready. You are building while you move.

And once you start, you will never look at your ideas the same way again.

Etsy in a Flash

Etsy used to feel like a place for people who could crochet, draw, or press flowers into handmade journals. And while that side of Etsy still exists, the platform has evolved into a massive marketplace for digital goods. That means you can create and sell something on Etsy without ever touching a printer, stocking inventory, or going to the post office.

The best part is that AI makes it ridiculously easy to get started, even if you have no design background and no idea what to sell. All you need is a simple concept, a clear offer, and a bit of time to build it out. Let me walk you through what that looked like the first time I tried it.

I had been using ChatGPT to brainstorm ideas for digital products. I wanted something lightweight but useful, something people could download and start using right away. After five minutes of prompting, I landed on the idea of a "daily writing warm-up sheet" designed for people who journal, blog, or write creatively but often get stuck starting.

Once I had the idea, I asked the AI to generate a few variations of the daily layout. It gave me prompts, questions, quote boxes, even section titles. I copied the best parts and started laying them out in Canva using one of their free templates. I added a title, tweaked the colors, and exported the final version as a PDF. Total time spent building the product was under two hours.

Next, I used AI again to write the product description. I asked it to generate a short paragraph explaining who it was for, what made it helpful, and how someone could use it daily. I edited a few lines to sound more like me, but most of it was ready to go. I uploaded the PDF to Etsy, added my description and a cover image, set the price at five dollars, and hit publish.

It sold on the second day.

Not because it was the most brilliant product ever, but because I followed through. I took an idea from concept to store page without trying to make it perfect. I used the tools to remove friction. I let good enough be good enough.

That one product led me to try a few more. I made printable planners for content creators, a digital vision board kit, and a goal-setting template built for freelancers. Each one took about one to three hours to complete. Some sold better than others. But every listing gave me more confidence, more feedback, and more clarity on what kind of things people actually wanted.

If you are thinking about trying Etsy, do not wait until your design is flawless or your idea feels unique. Start with something useful and simple. Let AI help you shape the offer. Ask it for product title ideas, SEO-friendly tags, marketing blurbs, and sample customer questions. Use Canva or Adobe Express to design a clean, professional-looking layout. You can even generate icons and illustrations with image tools like Bing or Firefly if you want to add personality.

Once you upload your product, let it sit. Post about it if you want, or just let Etsy's search engine do its thing. Track what happens. Tweak your listing based on what you learn. And then do it again, better and faster.

You do not need a shop full of products to get started. You need one product that teaches you how the process works. One listing that proves you can create something and put it into the world. After that, every next step gets easier.

Etsy rewards consistency, not perfection. The algorithm favors sellers who update often, add listings regularly, and keep experimenting. AI makes all of that easier. It removes the mental weight of starting and gives you the momentum to keep going.

You might not go viral overnight. You might only make a few dollars in the beginning. But that is all part of the game. You are building skill. You are learning how to package value. And you are creating assets that work while you sleep.

This is not about building a full-time income in a weekend. It is about learning how to turn your ideas into income streams with the tools you already have. One product. One hour. One store page.

That is all it takes to begin.

Writing for Bucks

If you have ever written something and thought, I wish I could get paid for this, you are not alone. Writing is one of the oldest creative hustles out there, and now with AI in the mix, it is more accessible than ever. You do not have to be an expert, a novelist, or a content marketing machine. You just need to be willing to show up, shape ideas, and deliver value with words. The internet has an endless appetite for writing, and AI is the tool that helps you meet that demand without burning out.

The first step is getting clear on what kind of writing people will pay for. Businesses are always looking for blog posts, email copy, product descriptions, and website content. Creators and coaches need help drafting newsletters, social posts, and bios.

New brands want story-driven about pages and taglines that pop. And the truth is, a lot of those people do not want to write it themselves.

They want someone who can make words sound good and deliver on time. AI makes that part easy. It helps you generate drafts, improve flow, and polish your final product without starting from scratch. You still need to bring your voice, your instincts, and your ability to shape the message, but the heavy lifting is already halfway done before you sit down.

Let me give you a real example. A friend of mine wanted to make some extra cash but didn't consider herself a writer. She was good with words but always froze at the blank page. I showed her how to use ChatGPT to write content for small business websites. She started by offering simple services on Fiverr. Things like writing product blurbs, homepage copy, and short blog intros. Each time, she would ask the AI to give her three variations, then pick the best one and personalize it. Within a few weeks, she was making consistent side income. Not huge numbers, but enough to see what was possible.

The best part is that she got faster with every project. The more she used AI to speed up the early draft stage, the more she could focus on making her writing stand out. And because she wasn't drained by the process, she actually started enjoying it.

That same path is open to anyone. You can start by offering writing services on freelance platforms. Or you can go independent and offer micro-packages on your website or through social media. You can even write your own digital products like guides, templates, or mini e-books using AI to structure and format them. If you are writing something valuable, someone out there is willing to pay for it.

To get started, think about the kind of writing that feels easiest to you. Maybe it is casual blog-style content. Maybe it is clean and snappy email copy. Maybe it is storytelling that makes people feel something. Use AI to help with outlines, variations, editing, and repackaging your work for different audiences. Ask it to write in specific tones, formats, or for different types of clients. The more you explore, the more confident you will get.

And once you have a few samples, you can use those to pitch. Offer value first. Show how your writing helps solve a problem or save time. You do not need a portfolio full of published pieces. You just need a few solid examples that show you know how to write something someone actually needs.

It is worth saying that writing for money does not have to mean client work forever. Many writers eventually use their skills to launch their own content businesses. That might look like a paid newsletter, a blog with affiliate links, a digital zine, or even serialized fiction. Once you know how to write consistently and connect with an audience, you are in control of where it goes.

AI does not replace your voice. It helps you get to your voice faster. It keeps you moving through the rough parts and lets you focus on what matters. The connection. The insight. The value.

If writing has always been your thing, this is the time to lean in. If it has never felt like your thing, now is the time to give it another shot. The tools are here. The demand is real. And the possibilities are wide open.

You are already a writer. You just need a way to get paid for it.

Try This Now

If you have ever thought about starting something but kept putting it off, this is your chance to change that. You do not need a full plan. You do not need a brand name, a strategy, or a five-year vision. All you need is a small idea, a bit of time, and the decision to just try.

This challenge is designed to help you move fast and get something out into the world. It is not about chasing perfect. It is about creating momentum. Think of it as a weekend experiment with low risk and real potential.

Start by picking one thing you have already explored in this book. Maybe it is a writing tool you enjoyed. Maybe you made an AI-generated image that sparked an idea. Maybe you liked the idea of digital products or short services. Choose one thread. Trust your instinct.

Next, define your offer. Keep it small. Maybe it is a five-dollar downloadable worksheet. Maybe it is a custom AI-generated story delivered by email. Maybe it is a one-page website with a simple booking link for writing bios or product blurbs. You are not launching a company. You are launching a test.

Use AI to help you write the product description. Ask it for a few variations. Mix and match the parts you like. Do the same for the name. Let the AI give you fun, clever, or professional options. Pick one that feels right and roll with it.

Create a visual using a tool like Canva, Firefly, or Bing Image Creator. This does not need to be fancy. A single image with clean text is enough. If you want, you can create a mockup of your product in action. Again, this is about progress, not perfection.

Now upload your offer somewhere. Etsy works great for digital goods. Gumroad is another fast option. If you are offering a service, create a Google Form, a Notion page, or even just a pinned post on Instagram or TikTok. It does not have to be a full storefront. It just has to exist.

Once it is live, share it with someone. One person is enough. Post it. Text it. DM a friend. Say something like, hey, I made this. Let me know what you think. That moment, when you send something out, is when everything changes. You go from idea mode to builder mode.

You do not need it to go viral. You just need one person to react. To click. To download. To ask a question. That is how you get real feedback. That is how you learn what to do next.

You might update the listing. You might change the title. You might turn one download into five or ten. Or you might realize you want to try something different. Any of those outcomes are a win.

This is the heart of building a side hustle with AI. You do not need to wait until you have it all figured out. You start, learn, and keep moving. The tools are here to make everything faster. Your creativity makes it real.

Try something now. Give it a day or a weekend. Let yourself be curious. Let yourself be a little scrappy. You will be amazed how good it feels to put something into the world that started as a random idea in your head. You have more value to offer than you think. And the only way to prove that to yourself is to try. This is your launch moment.

Let's see what happens.

Chapter 9: Growing Up with AI

Up to this point, we've used AI to create, explore, and experiment. You've seen how it can help you write, make art, build music, and test side hustles. But creativity isn't the only thing AI can amplify. It can also support the way you think, grow, and evolve.

This chapter is about using AI not as a tool for output, but as a tool for self-reflection. It's about how artificial intelligence can help you get to know yourself better, develop stronger habits, untangle emotions, and stay focused when life gets chaotic. Think of it as having a pocket-sized coach, therapist, journal, and hype squad all rolled into one.

You don't need to be in crisis mode to benefit from this. You might just be feeling scattered. You might be chasing too many things at once. You might have ideas but no direction. That's where AI can become surprisingly useful. It listens without judgment. It helps you organize thoughts. It pushes you to ask better questions and sometimes gives answers you didn't expect.

In this chapter, you'll learn how to use AI to check in with yourself, challenge your limiting beliefs, build better routines, and reframe your thinking. You'll see how simple prompts can lead to big shifts. You'll also get tools and exercises you can return to anytime your mindset starts to slip or your motivation runs low.

This is not about fixing yourself. It's about getting clear. Learning how to use AI as a mirror, a motivator, and a quiet guide. You don't need to become a different person. You just need to become more of who you already are.

Let's explore how AI can help you grow in the ways that matter most.

The Confidence Kick

Confidence is one of those things that feels solid when you have it and slippery when you don't. You might be great at something and still second-guess yourself. Or you might be trying something new and feeling like an imposter the whole way through. That inner voice, the one that says you're not ready or not good enough, loves to show up right when you're about to make a move. AI can't magically delete that voice, but it can help you change the conversation.

The first time I used AI to boost my own confidence, I wasn't even looking for that. I had opened ChatGPT to brainstorm headline ideas for a project I was stuck on. What came back were phrases I never would've written myself. They were bold, punchy, and weirdly exciting. I started laughing. Not because the results were perfect, but because they reminded me that my idea actually had potential. I just needed to look at it from a different angle.

That moment gave me a tiny push. A shift. Enough to keep going.

Since then, I've used AI to build confidence in all kinds of ways. When I feel uncertain about something I made, I'll paste it into a chat and ask for feedback in a supportive tone. I'll ask questions like, "What's strong about this?" or "How could this be useful to someone else?" The answers don't come with ego or agenda. They come with perspective.

And when I need motivation, I ask for it directly. "Write me a pep talk in the style of a mentor who believes in me." Or, "What's a reminder I might need to hear right now if I'm scared to launch something new?" You'd be surprised how often the response lands. It's like having a version of your best self in your corner, ready with a calm voice and a flashlight when things get dark.

But the real confidence kick comes from using AI to take action. Not just to think, but to move. Confidence grows when you make progress, when you follow through, when you hit publish or send or record. AI makes those steps easier. It clears the first few feet of the path so you can take the next one.

Let's say you want to post about something you're working on, but your brain starts throwing out all the usual doubts. What if it's dumb? What if no one cares? What if I mess it up? You can flip that by opening a chat and asking, "Can you help me write a short post that explains this idea in a friendly, confident way?" You take what comes back, tweak it, and suddenly the scary part is done. You are not frozen anymore.

Confidence isn't about pretending you know everything. It's about trusting yourself to figure it out. It's built through reps, through doing things even when your hands are shaking a little. AI gives you a safe place to practice. You can say, "What would this sound like if I said it with more clarity?" Or, "How would I explain this if I actually believed in myself?"

It doesn't take much. A better sentence. A clearer idea. A single win.

Over time, that adds up. You start showing up more. You take more creative risks. You post the thing you were afraid to post. You reach out to someone you admire. You pitch something you would have kept hidden in a notebook last year.

And yes, sometimes it still feels scary. But that fear doesn't get to run the show anymore. You've got tools. You've got perspective. You've got receipts. AI won't give you confidence. But it will help you build it. Word by word. Win by win.

You've got more in you than you think. Let's keep proving it.

Journal Hack

Journaling always sounded good in theory. Reflecting. Processing. Getting your thoughts out before they pile up in your chest or swirl around your brain at night. But like a lot of things that are good for you, it's easy to skip. You sit down, open a blank page, and suddenly your brain forgets how to talk. Or worse, you start writing the same three sentences over and over again, trying to sound insightful.

That's where the AI journal hack comes in.

Instead of facing a blank page, you use AI to meet you where you are. You treat it like a co-journaler, a prompt machine, or a mirror that gently asks the right questions when your own mind goes quiet.

Some days, I open a chat window and type something as simple as "Can you help me reflect on my week?" The AI will come back with questions. Not deep therapy questions, just simple ones. What energized you this week? What drained you? What's one thing you're proud of? What's something you'd like to do differently next time? I answer them in the same window, just typing out my thoughts as they come.

What happens is kind of magic. The friction disappears. I stop worrying about how I sound. I stop trying to write something smart or poetic. I just respond.

Other days, I'll ask for a specific kind of reflection. Like "Help me unpack this decision I'm struggling with," or "Guide me through a five-minute check-in to see why I'm feeling stuck." The AI becomes a sounding board, a tool for untangling whatever I'm holding inside.

If I'm feeling off but can't put my finger on why, I'll ask "Can you help me figure out what emotion I'm feeling and where it might be coming from?" Nine times out of ten, it gets me closer than I expected.

There are also days when I want to track progress. So I ask it to help me journal about my creative habits, or my mindset shifts over the past month. I might prompt it with "Let's review what changed for me in April," and it'll guide me through remembering what I tried, what worked, and what I want to build on.

This version of journaling works because it's fluid. There are no rules, no format, and no pressure to write a certain way. You're not writing for an audience. You're not building a streak. You're just being honest with yourself in the simplest way possible.

The best part is that you can return to it anytime. You can pick up where you left off. You can say, "Hey, remember last week when I said I was afraid to send that email? I finally did it," and the AI will reflect that back to you. You see your own growth in real time.

If you want to get even more structured, you can ask the AI to build you a custom journaling ritual. Ask it to create a five-minute morning routine or a ten-minute end-of-week reflection you can repeat. You can even save your favorite questions and revisit them every Sunday night.

Journaling doesn't have to look like pages of handwritten wisdom. Sometimes it's just a few lines that unlock clarity. Sometimes it's a quick exchange that turns your whole day around. Sometimes it's five minutes of dumping out the mental noise so you can get back to creating, living, moving.

AI doesn't replace the value of your inner voice. It just makes it easier to hear. And when your thoughts are all over the place, or nowhere at all, it gives you something to bounce off.

This isn't about doing it perfectly. It's about staying connected to yourself. Even in the middle of chaos. Especially in the middle of chaos. If traditional journaling hasn't worked for you, try the hack. Start with a question. Let the AI ask the next one. See what shows up.

You'll be surprised what's waiting to be said.

Dreams on Paper

a blur in the back of your mind that lights up when you hear a certain song or walk past the right kind of bookstore. The other is something you can look at, read, and return to. Something that makes your next step a little less foggy.

Getting your dreams on paper is a powerful act. It's also something most of us avoid. Not because we don't care, but because naming your dream feels risky. What if you name it and then fail? What if it feels too big or too small or too strange? What if it changes?

AI gives you a way around that fear. It creates space to explore your ideas without pressure or judgment. You can ask it questions. You can test out future paths. You can describe the feeling of what you want before you even know the exact shape.

I've used AI in this way more than I expected. Sometimes I open a chat window and type, "Can you help me write a vision for what I want my creative life to look like in a year?" The response usually starts with a broad description. Then I ask for more detail. What kind of projects am I working on? Who am I collaborating with? What does my daily routine look like? The picture gets sharper each time I ask.

Sometimes I'll go the other way and say, "Describe a version of my life five years from now if I never take risks creatively." That one hits harder. It's not meant to scare me, but to wake me up a little. It reminds me that action matters. That the window of time is always shifting.

If you're not sure what your dream looks like, start with the pieces. Ask the AI, "What kind of creative paths fit someone who enjoys storytelling and visual design but doesn't like working alone?" Or say, "Give me examples of work that feels adventurous, meaningful, and a little rebellious." You'll get job ideas, project types, and directions to explore. Some will feel off. Some will feel like maybe, just maybe, they're close to something true.

The more you explore, the more you'll feel it when something clicks. That's the moment to lean in.

Once you have a rough idea, start shaping it. Ask for help writing a future bio. Ask the AI to describe a day in your ideal creative life. Or build a manifesto with phrases like "I want to make things that…" and "I believe in work that…" Let the sentences evolve. Let them feel honest.

The goal here is not to carve something in stone. The goal is to give your dream enough form that you can work with it. You don't need a business plan. You don't need five clear goals. You just need a direction. A vision that belongs to you and no one else.

When you write that down, even in messy sentences, you change something. The dream stops floating. It starts to land.

You can revisit this process anytime. Once a month. Once a season. Once a year. Each time, it will reflect where you are and where you're growing. It's a map, not a contract. You get to revise it as many times as you want.

And if you ever lose track of what you want, just ask the AI what you told it before. Paste in your old vision and say, "Can you remind me why I wanted this?" Sometimes the words that come back will feel more like you than you expected.

That's the power of getting your dreams on paper. They become something you can carry, shape, and speak out loud. Even if they're still evolving. Even if they're still a little wild.

They're yours now. And that makes them real.

Try This Now

You've seen how AI can support reflection, boost confidence, and help you name what matters. Now it's time to use that momentum for a simple but powerful challenge. One that's less about productivity and more about clarity. Less about doing more and more about understanding yourself better.

Set aside fifteen minutes. You don't need a notebook or fancy app. Just open an AI chat window and show up as you are.

Start by typing this: I'd like to reflect on where I'm at creatively and where I want to go. Can you guide me through that with a few thoughtful questions?

Let the AI take the lead for a moment. You might get questions about your current habits, your recent wins, or what lights you up when you're not thinking about results. Answer the ones that hit. Skip the ones that don't. Let it be a conversation, not a checklist.

If you want more structure, ask it to break your reflection into three parts. Where you've been, where you are, and where you want to go. This helps create a natural flow. It shows you the progress you've already made, the patterns you're sitting in now, and the future you're starting to shape.

Once you've gone through a few rounds of back-and-forth, ask the AI to help you summarize what came up. Say something like, Based on what I've shared, can you help me write a personal mission statement or creative vision I can return to when I feel stuck?

You'll get a paragraph or two. Some of it will feel close to home. Some of it might feel off. That's okay. Tweak the parts that don't sound like you. Highlight the parts that make you sit up a little straighter. You're not just writing a reflection. You're shaping language that reminds you who you are when you're at your best.

If you want to go further, ask the AI to help you design a creative ritual or daily check-in based on your vision. Something short and sustainable. Something you can return to on days when your brain feels scrambled or your confidence disappears. The best rituals are the ones that anchor you back to yourself without requiring a big performance.

This is your foundation. You've taken your inner thoughts and brought them to the surface. You've looked at where you've been and where you want to go. You've turned abstract feelings into something you can actually use.

You can return to this process anytime. It's always available. There's no badge, no grade, no leaderboard. Just you showing up for yourself in a deeper way than you did the day before.

That's what growth looks like. Not a sudden transformation. A quiet shift. A new sentence. A clearer answer. Try this now. See what comes through.

You might be surprised by what you already know.

Chapter 10: AI and Me – A Creative Tag Team

By now, you've seen how AI can do a lot. It can help you brainstorm, create, write, reflect, and build. But the real magic isn't in the tech itself. It's in what happens when you start thinking of AI not as a tool, but as a creative partner. Not something that replaces your ideas, but something that sharpens them.

That's what this chapter is about. Learning how to work with AI in a way that feels like collaboration instead of delegation. It's where you stop asking, "What can it do for me?" and start asking, "How can we do this together?"

A lot of people get nervous here. They worry that using AI will dilute their voice, flatten their originality, or make their work feel less personal. But what I've found is the opposite. When you're intentional about how you use it, AI actually helps you get to your voice faster. It clears the noise. It speeds up the hard parts. And it holds space for you to play, refine, and go deeper.

This chapter will show you how to balance input and intuition. How to use AI for the heavy lifting while still making sure the final product sounds and feels like you. You'll see how to mix your natural creative process with what the tech offers, without losing the spark that makes your work worth sharing.

Because creativity doesn't come from having all the answers. It comes from knowing how to dance with uncertainty. And AI, when used right, is an incredible dance partner.

Let's learn how to move together.

Why I'm Still the Boss

The moment you start creating with AI, you'll notice something strange. The tool can generate five variations of an idea in less than a minute. It can write paragraphs that sound polished. It can suggest storylines, product names, headlines, hashtags, color palettes, character arcs, and calls to action. It can even make you second-guess yourself a little. Like, if the machine can do this so fast, what's the point of me?

That feeling is real. And also, it's a trap. Because the point of you isn't speed. It's judgment.

You are the filter. You are the taste. You are the one who knows when something is close but still not right. You're the one who can tell when a sentence sounds flat or a design feels empty or a story doesn't land the way it should. AI might give you more options, but it can't tell you which one is worth running with. That's your job.

There was a stretch when I started relying too much on the tools. I'd plug in a prompt, scroll through the results, and pick the one that sounded the smartest. But when I read it back later, I didn't recognize myself in the work. It was technically correct. It even looked good on the surface. But it didn't have my rhythm, my edges, my point of view. It felt like a copy of a copy.

That's when I shifted my mindset.

I stopped treating AI like a writer or an artist. I started treating it like a collaborator who was great at first drafts and wild suggestions but not good at knowing when something *feels* right. I stopped expecting it to finish things. I started asking it to *start* things so I could shape them.

Now when I use it, I remind myself that my gut is the final editor. Not the algorithm. I keep my own tone close. I ask myself, does this sound like me? Would I say it this way? Is there something here I want to push further or cut entirely? I use AI to get moving, not to define the destination. It also means knowing when not to use it.

Sometimes I sit with an idea before I open a chat window. I write the first few lines on my own, even if they're slow or clumsy. That's how I stay connected to my instincts. If I use AI too soon, I risk shortcutting the part of my brain that's trying to wrestle something out. The struggle is part of the signal. It helps me know what I care about.

Other times, I'll generate ten options and throw them all out. Not because they're bad, but because none of them feel aligned. That's okay too. Just because AI gives you something doesn't mean you have to use it. You're not wasting time. You're exploring.

Being the boss of your creativity doesn't mean doing everything alone. It means knowing which parts of the process matter most to *you*, and protecting those. Maybe that's your voice. Maybe that's your storytelling style. Maybe it's your color choices or your message or the way you talk to your audience. Whatever it is, keep it centered. Let AI work around *you*, not the other way around.

The real power of this partnership is how it lets you move faster without losing your signature. It helps you show up more, but still sound like yourself. It helps you go deeper, because you're not stuck in the early chaos. You can focus your energy where it matters.

You're still the creative director of everything you make. You call the shots. You shape the tone. You say when it's done.

No matter how smart the tool gets, that part belongs to you.

Mixing It Old School

For all the speed and flash of AI, sometimes the best ideas still come when your hands are off the keyboard. There's something about old school tools—pen, paper, sticky notes, notebooks—that lets your brain move in a different way. Slower. Weirder. Sometimes smarter.

When I first started using AI in my creative routine, I went all in. Every idea started in a chat window. Every headline was AI-assisted. Every draft got cleaned up by a bot. It felt efficient, and it was. But after a while, I noticed something missing. My work was starting to feel flat. Too clean. Too safe. So I went back to basics.

I started sketching ideas in a notebook before opening any apps. I started using index cards to map out story beats instead of relying on generated outlines. I scribbled brand names and taglines in the margins of old receipts. And once I had something rough, *then* I brought it into the AI chat to explore or improve it.

That changed everything.

Instead of letting the tool guide me from the start, I was guiding it. I was bringing my half-formed, messy, human ideas to the table and using AI to sharpen them. That small shift gave me better results and helped me stay connected to the part of the process that made me feel like a real creator.

There's something about writing by hand or brainstorming on paper that slows you down just enough to notice details. Your brain makes strange jumps. You connect thoughts you wouldn't have typed. You take your time.

And it turns out, AI actually works better when you give it raw material that comes from that slower, more analog place. You can say, "Here's a list of phrases I wrote during a brainstorm. Can you help me remix them into something punchier?" Or, "I scribbled this tagline idea while walking. Can you give me variations that keep the same energy?"

When you start with old school input, the AI output feels more alive. Because it's building from *you*, not just from the prompt template it's seen a thousand times.

I've started creating a routine around this. I set a timer for ten minutes and write whatever comes to mind about an idea. No formatting, no pressure. Then I take the best parts and paste them into the AI chat to explore further. Sometimes I draw a logo concept by hand before generating polished versions online. Sometimes I write a messy paragraph and ask the AI to rewrite it in the tone of a friend hyping me up. The final result is a blend. Human spark, machine polish.

Mixing it old school doesn't mean rejecting tech. It means remembering that your best creative energy doesn't always live in the digital space. Sometimes you need the scribble. The pause. The blank page that doesn't glow. It's easy to forget this when everything is fast and optimized. But slowing down is where some of your best stuff hides.

You might be surprised what happens when you take five minutes to sketch before you prompt. Or when you brainstorm on paper before you ask the AI for ideas. That little bit of friction creates space. And in that space, your brain does its best work.

So yes, use the tools. But don't be afraid to step away from the screen and let your brain wander in the margins. You don't have to choose one or the other. The real power comes from mixing the two. Old school mess. New school speed. That's the combo.

And it's all yours to play with.

No Robot Voice Here

You've probably seen it. That polished, lifeless tone that sneaks into AI-generated content. It sounds smart on the surface but completely forgettable underneath. It's the kind of voice that uses words like "leverage" and "synergy" in places where a real person would just say "use" or "work together." It's clean. It's consistent. And it has no soul. That's the robot voice. And it's everywhere.

But it doesn't have to be in your work. Because the truth is, AI only sounds robotic when you let it. Left on its own, it will default to safe, neutral, and formal. That's what the internet has trained it to do. But if you're clear and intentional about what you want, you can steer it back to something that sounds like *you*.

This took me a while to figure out. Early on, I'd ask the AI to help me write things like bios or product blurbs. What came back was fine, but it didn't hit. It sounded like someone trying to sound important. So I started getting more specific. Instead of saying, "Write a product description," I'd say, "Write this like I'm talking to a friend who's on the fence about trying it." Or, "Write this in a playful, slightly nerdy tone with short sentences and no buzzwords."

Everything changed.

The writing got lighter. More natural. More me. The robot voice faded. And in its place was something that sounded like the kind of stuff I'd actually say out loud. Now, whenever I generate content with AI, I give it a vibe to match. I'll paste in a paragraph I wrote and say, "Match this tone." Or I'll explain my writing style in a sentence. I might say, "I write with short bursts, vivid examples, and a slightly sarcastic edge." The more I guide the tone, the better the results.

If you don't know your writing voice yet, that's okay. You can use AI to help you find it. Try pasting in three things you've written that felt true to you. Ask the AI to analyze the tone. What patterns does it notice? What words or rhythms show up again and again? Then ask it to help you write new content using those same qualities.

Over time, your voice becomes clearer. You start to recognize when something sounds like you and when it doesn't. That instinct sharpens. And once it does, you'll start editing more confidently. You'll stop accepting whatever the AI gives you and start shaping it, sentence by sentence, until it feels honest. That's the real work. Not just generating content, but *owning* it.

This matters because your voice is your fingerprint. It's what makes people read your writing and feel like they're hearing from a real person, not a help desk or a press release. It's the reason people keep coming back. Not because your ideas are always perfect, but because your perspective feels human. And in a world filling up with AI-written everything, your human edge is your advantage.

You don't have to write like a poet. You don't have to be clever in every sentence. You just have to sound like someone worth listening to. Someone who cares. Someone who's showing up as themselves, not as a placeholder.

So when you use AI, make it work with your voice, not over it. Tell it how you speak. Tell it how you *don't* want to sound. Tell it what words you'd never use, what phrases make you cringe, what tone feels like you at your best. Protect your weirdness. Keep your rhythm. Let your voice lead.

No robot voice here.

Try This Now

If you've made it this far, you're not just experimenting with AI. You're starting to own the process. You've learned how to bring your creativity into the mix, how to shape what the tool gives you, and how to keep your voice front and center. Now it's time to test that in the simplest way possible: by making something small that feels like *you*.

This challenge isn't about scale. It's about clarity. Your goal is to create one piece of content—written, visual, or audio—that uses AI to assist but not define it. Something where your fingerprints are all over the final result.

Start by choosing a format you enjoy. Maybe it's a short post. Maybe it's a quote card with a caption. Maybe it's a short video script or a single-page story. Don't pick something big. Pick something light, low-stakes, and fun to make.

Now open a chat window and describe what you want to create. Be specific about tone. Tell it how you want it to sound or feel. Ask for a draft or a few options. Don't just copy and paste. Read it. React to it. Rewrite the lines that feel off. Make it yours.

If you want to go deeper, paste in a short paragraph you've written in your natural voice and ask the AI to mimic the tone.

Then use that tone to generate something new. Keep what fits. Edit the rest.

The goal here is not perfection. It's alignment. You want to finish with something that you're proud to share because it reflects your perspective, your energy, and your creative flavor.

Once it's done, share it somewhere. Anywhere. Post it, send it to a friend, or just save it in a folder with a name that makes you smile. Give it a title. Call it your remix. Your blend. Your first real tag-team creation.

You can repeat this anytime. It's one of the fastest ways to stay in touch with your voice and build your skills. The more you practice this kind of collaboration, the easier it gets. You'll start knowing exactly how to prompt for what you need. You'll recognize what's missing without second-guessing. You'll start editing like a pro without overthinking.

And when people see your work, they won't say, "This sounds AI-written." They'll say, "This sounds like you." That's the power of doing it your way. So go make something now. Let the AI help, but let your gut lead. Say it the way only you can. And remember, you're not outsourcing your creativity. You're expanding it.

You're the voice. AI's just the echo.

Chapter 11: Taming the AI Beast

Up until now, we've been in creation mode. We've explored the wild side of what's possible when you let AI into your creative world. You've brainstormed, built, published, reflected, and maybe even launched something new. But there's another side to this tech—one that's not so shiny. AI can be too much.

Too many options. Too many directions. Too many tabs open and voices whispering in your ear. The tool that once felt like a superpower can quickly turn into a source of pressure, noise, or straight-up burnout.

This chapter is about that side. The part where AI overwhelms instead of supports. The moments when you start to feel like you're not creating anymore, just generating. The temptation to chase output over meaning. The creeping feeling that maybe your voice is getting lost in the flood.

Taming the beast doesn't mean walking away from the tools. It means learning how to set boundaries with them. It means knowing when to pause, when to trust yourself more than the machine, and how to stay grounded in your own creative energy. It means treating AI like a collaborator, not a boss.

You're going to learn how to use less when less is what you need. How to spot the signs of creative overload. How to filter through noise and get back to flow. And how to protect your voice, your time, and your headspace. Because creative power isn't just about how much you can make. It's about knowing what matters, and having the clarity to keep showing up for it.

Let's take a breath, zoom out, and get back to what's real.

When It's Too Much

There's a moment that sneaks up on a lot of people when they start working with AI. At first, it's all speed and magic. You're generating ideas faster than ever. You're writing blog posts in half the time. You're making stuff that looks like it came from a pro studio. Everything feels like a superpower.

Then one day, you look at your screen and feel nothing. No spark. No direction. Just a pile of good-enough options and a tired brain.

This is what happens when AI turns into noise.

It's easy to mistake motion for meaning. You're generating more, so it *must* be progress. You're producing faster, so it *must* be working. But the truth is, creativity doesn't always move in straight lines. Sometimes it needs stillness. Sometimes it needs slowness. And sometimes, the smartest thing you can do is stop asking the machine for answers and start asking yourself what you actually want to say.

I've had moments where I opened five AI tabs at once. One for headlines. One for visuals. One for captions. One for outlines. One for brainstorming names. What started as support quickly became overwhelm. I was drowning in options, none of which felt fully mine.

And the problem wasn't the tools. The problem was me forgetting to pause.

When you rely on AI too heavily, you can lose the thread. The thread is your vision. Your taste. Your voice. The deeper reason behind why you're creating in the first place. If you skip that step, you end up building things that look right but feel off. Projects that check all the boxes but leave you feeling weirdly disconnected. That disconnection is a signal.

It means you've reached the edge of what the tools can do for you. And it's time to come back to center. If you feel overwhelmed by all the options AI throws at you, close the tabs. Step away from the feed. Grab a pen or take a walk. Ask yourself a few grounding questions. What do I actually want to make right now? What part of this project matters most to me? What do I want someone to feel when they see or hear or read this?

You might not get perfect answers, but you'll start to hear yourself again. That's the part AI can't give you. That's the part that makes the rest of it work.

Overload doesn't just come from too many ideas. It comes from skipping intention. When everything's possible, you need something to hold onto. Not a system. Not a script. Just something real.

That realness might be a phrase that feels true. A topic that lights you up. A weird little visual in your head that won't let go. That's your anchor. Hold onto it. Let the AI support *that*, not drown it out.

Sometimes, when I'm deep in a creative fog, I'll type something like this into my AI chat: I feel overwhelmed by too many options. Can you help me ask better questions so I can get clear again? And instead of asking it to solve everything, I let it help me slow down. I treat it less like a productivity engine and more like a sounding board. That's where it shines.

The truth is, there's no medal for doing the most. No prize for how many variations you can generate. The real win is when you make something that feels like it came from the part of you that still believes in wonder. The part that's not trying to beat the algorithm, but trying to connect with someone. Even if that someone is just you.

If you're in a place where everything feels like too much, that's not failure. That's your creative system asking for a reset. That's the moment to trust yourself more than the screen.

Because the machine can give you content. But only you can give it meaning.

Fear Factor

There's a quiet kind of fear that creeps in when you start using AI seriously. It doesn't show up with flashing lights. It doesn't always speak in full sentences. But it's there, humming underneath your progress, asking uncomfortable questions.

What if this idea isn't mine?
What if I'm cheating?
What if people can tell?

Even when you're doing the work—editing, refining, steering the output—part of your brain might whisper that it doesn't count. That maybe you've lost something by not starting from scratch. That maybe this tool you're using to go further is also exposing how far you couldn't go alone. That fear can get in the way.

It's the fear of being fake. The fear of being called out. The fear that your creativity isn't real if it's been assisted. And here's the truth. That fear is understandable. But it's also not the full story.

Using AI doesn't make your work less valuable. It just changes the process. Creativity has always evolved alongside the tools we use. Painters used new pigments. Musicians used synthesizers. Writers used spellcheck and editors and laptops instead of typewriters. Every shift brought out the same fear. And every time, creativity adapted.

What matters isn't whether you used AI. It's how you used it. What you brought to it. What you made out of the raw material. The voice behind the edits. The perspective behind the choices. You're not cheating. You're creating with support.

Still, the fear sticks sometimes. Especially when you're sharing something that started with an AI draft. You might wonder if people will dismiss it. If they'll assume it was auto-generated and therefore empty. And that fear might make you play smaller. Soften your voice. Apologize before anyone even asks a question. But here's the thing. People connect with honesty, not origin stories.

If your work speaks clearly, moves someone, makes them think, or gives them something to hold onto, they won't care where the first draft came from. They'll care that it landed. That it mattered. That you cared enough to make it worth reading, watching, hearing. If you're struggling with fear around using AI, here's what helps. Stop hiding it. Own it.

Say, I use AI to generate rough ideas so I can spend more time shaping the final product. Say, This image started with an AI concept and I layered in my own design. Say, I co-created this with a tool because it helped me work through a creative block and find something real.

You don't have to defend the process. But the more transparent you are with yourself, the more confident you'll feel. The fear fades when you stop pretending and start owning your rhythm.

Another fear that can show up is the fear of dependency. You might start asking, What if I forget how to write without it? What if I lose my creative instincts? What if I need this tool too much? That's a valid concern. But the answer isn't to stop using AI. It's to stay aware.

Keep writing your own messy drafts sometimes. Sketch without prompts. Think before you type. Use the tool, but also step away from it. Test your creative muscles without the crutch. You'll find they're stronger than you remember. Fear thrives in silence. In the spaces where you don't examine it.

So name it. Talk about it. Ask yourself what part of it is true and what part is just old programming. You're not here to create in a vacuum. You're here to make something that feels honest. And if AI is part of that process, so be it.

This is new territory for everyone. The rules are being written as we speak.

And in this moment, the most important thing you can do isn't to have all the answers. It's to keep showing up. To keep creating. To keep shaping your voice, your path, your body of work. Even when it's scary.

Especially then.

Quick and Dirty Tips

By now, you've probably felt both sides of AI. The thrill of what it can do, and the drag of what it can do too much of. It's fast, yes. But it's also a firehose. And if you're not careful, it can blast you with so many options, so much noise, that your own instincts get buried under all the "maybe."

This section is here to help with that. Think of it as a creative reset. The things I do when I feel overwhelmed, uninspired, or a little too caught up in the machine. None of these are complicated. But they work.

First, when you feel stuck, stop generating. That sounds obvious, but it's not always easy to do. When you hit a wall, the temptation is to keep asking AI for more. More options. More prompts. More answers. But sometimes the real problem isn't a lack of input. It's too much of it. The more you pile on, the harder it is to hear your own voice. So pause. Step away from the screen. Go analog for a bit. Write one line by hand. Doodle your idea. Talk it out with someone who gets you. Do anything that breaks the loop.

Second, get specific. AI works better when you ask better questions. Instead of asking for ten names, ask for ten names that sound playful but nostalgic, or that could fit a 90s-themed candle brand. Don't ask for blog titles. Ask for a headline that sounds like your favorite writer would say it. The more specific you are, the less generic the output. And the less editing you have to do later.

Third, pick one idea and follow it through. AI will tempt you with infinite detours. You'll get one good result, then ask for five more versions. Then you'll start comparing. Then second-guessing. Before you know it, you're ten layers deep and can't remember what the point was. When something feels close to right, stop digging. Use it. Shape it. Ship it.

Fourth, limit your sessions. Don't make every project an AI marathon. Give yourself a container. Twenty minutes to brainstorm. Fifteen minutes to generate ideas. Ten minutes to remix. If you stay inside the fence, you'll be more focused, less frazzled, and way more likely to finish something. Creative energy has limits. Protect yours.

Fifth, keep your weird. AI will often steer things toward the middle. The average. The default. You'll start noticing your content feels cleaner, more readable, but also less *you*. When that happens, ask yourself, what was the weird little twist I was going to add before the tool polished it out? Put that back in. Keep the line that sounds offbeat. Keep the image that doesn't quite fit. That's the part people remember.

And finally, talk to yourself in the process. Literally. Out loud. Say what you're trying to do. Say what's missing. Say what you're afraid of. You'd be surprised how often your brain already knows the answer—you just need to give it the floor for a second. If you're using AI in a chat format, type it out like you're talking to a collaborator. Say, I think I'm close but I don't love this part. Can we try again with more attitude? That small shift turns the tool into a teammate.

You don't need a system to use AI well. You need awareness. Enough awareness to know when you're creating something that feels true and when you're just filling space. Enough awareness to pause when your brain says it's done, even if the tool wants to keep going.

Your creativity isn't a machine. It's a rhythm. A flow. A pattern that includes rest and mistakes and resistance and breakthroughs. AI can help you move through that rhythm faster. But it can't replace it.

So when things feel heavy, remember this isn't about being a content factory. This is about making things that matter to you. One idea. One page. One post.

Done is better than perfect, and done with heart beats polished and hollow every time.

Try This Now

You don't need a full digital detox to find your footing again. You just need a moment. One simple reset to remind yourself that the tools don't lead—you do. This exercise is for anyone feeling scattered, numb, overloaded, or just creatively foggy after too much prompting and too little connection.

Start with silence. No AI. No tabs. No distractions. Just grab a notebook or open a blank page and take five minutes to answer one question: What do I actually want to make right now?

Don't try to sound clever. Don't write what you think you're supposed to make. Just be honest. Maybe it's a poem. Maybe it's a weird story. Maybe it's a landing page for a half-formed business idea. Maybe it's nothing at all—just a need to take a breath. That counts too.

Once you have that answer, write a few messy lines about why it matters. Why this thing. Why now. What are you hoping to say, feel, or figure out by making it?

After you've grounded yourself, now—and only now—bring in AI. Ask it to help you get started, but frame the ask based on what you wrote. Say, I'm working on a short letter to future me.

I want it to feel personal, a little funny, and a little sad. Can you help me write an opening line that captures that mix?

Or, I've been thinking about starting a project about creative burnout. Can you help me outline a blog post that feels honest, not preachy? The goal is to use the tool like a flashlight, not a GPS. You already know where you're going. You're just asking for a little help seeing the next few feet.

Keep the session short. Fifteen to twenty minutes max. Don't open five windows. Don't spiral into ten variations. Use what works. Save what sparks something. Let the rest go. When you're done, ask yourself one more thing: Did this feel like mine?

Not perfect. Not polished. Just real.

If the answer is yes, you're doing it right. If the answer is no, go back to the part you wrote by hand. The messy start. The part where your gut showed up. That's the voice you're trying to follow.

You can repeat this reset anytime. Weekly. Monthly. On the days you feel like you're just going through the motions. It's a way of pausing the noise and remembering why you started making things in the first place.

Because you are not here to crank out content. You're here to connect. With yourself. With others. With whatever small truth you're trying to say out loud. The tools are powerful. But you are the point.

So try this now, reset the rhythm, reclaim your flow.

Chapter 12: AI Writing Bootcamp

You don't need to be a writer to use words well. You don't need to love writing to be good at it. But no matter what kind of creator you are, writing will always find its way into your world. Product descriptions. Instagram captions. Email newsletters. Sales pages. Blog posts. Journal entries. Every idea eventually needs to be communicated.

This chapter is here to help you do that with less friction and more flow.

Think of it as a writing bootcamp, but without the drills or the yelling. Just smart, practical ways to use AI to break through blocks, shape your ideas, and write in a voice that feels like yours. Whether you're writing for an audience, for clients, or for yourself, this is where you get to experiment with speed and structure without sacrificing soul.

We're going to walk through how to use AI for rough drafts, how to refine your tone, how to write in different formats, and how to stay consistent without sounding copy-paste. You'll see how to collaborate with AI in a way that sharpens your instincts instead of softening your edge.

By the end of this chapter, you'll have a repeatable writing system that doesn't feel robotic. You'll be able to generate first drafts fast, polish them with intention, and ship work that still sounds like you on your best day. And if you've ever said, "I hate writing," this might be the chapter that changes your mind.

Let's get into it.

ChatGPT Confessions

The first time I wrote with ChatGPT, I thought I was cheating. I had a blank screen, a half-decent idea, and no momentum. I typed a few instructions, something like, "Write an intro paragraph about the future of creativity." And boom—there it was. A fully formed, polished opening that looked like it belonged in a magazine.

I hated it.

Not because it was bad. It was clean, even inspiring in that vague way marketing copy can be. But it didn't feel like me. It was like watching someone wear a perfectly tailored jacket and realizing it looked great but didn't smell like your closet. The words were fine. They just weren't mine.

That was the moment I understood something important. AI could write for me, but it couldn't write *as* me. Not unless I trained it. Not unless I made it listen first.

I started experimenting. Instead of asking for paragraphs, I asked it to finish my sentences. I gave it pieces of my actual writing and asked it to match the rhythm. I started giving it more context, more tone, more personality. When I said "funny," I didn't mean sitcom funny. I meant dry, slightly unhinged, with a little nerd energy. When I said "casual," I didn't mean lazy. I meant human, like a voice note to a friend.

And when I got specific, the results got better. Not perfect. But closer. And I stopped feeling like I was cheating. I started feeling like I was jamming with a collaborator who had unlimited energy and no ego.

There were still days when it missed. Days when everything sounded flat or too polished or weirdly fake-deep. That's part of it. AI doesn't have moods, but you do. And sometimes the gap between what you're trying to say and what it gives you is wide enough to make you want to throw your laptop across the room. But that's not the tool's fault. That's just the process.

What surprised me most wasn't how fast it could write. It was how it made me braver. I'd ask it to try something I wouldn't dare say on my own. A bolder headline. A riskier joke. A sharper take. Sometimes it worked. Sometimes it bombed. But just seeing it written out gave me something to react to. Something to shape. It pulled the idea out of my head and onto the page, where I could finally deal with it.

That's the power of using AI to write. It's not about skipping the hard parts. It's about removing the friction between the idea and the expression. You still have to bring the spark. You still have to choose what stays, what changes, what gets cut. But you don't have to start from zero every time.

It doesn't mean you're less of a writer. It means you've learned how to use the tools that make writing more doable. And once you get used to that rhythm, something clicks.

You stop overthinking. You stop polishing before you've even drafted. You stop staring at the cursor waiting for inspiration to strike like lightning. Instead, you move. You build momentum. You work with the words instead of wrestling them into submission.

Now, I treat ChatGPT like a writing buddy who's always down to brainstorm, test ideas, clean up sentences, or throw twenty bad suggestions at the wall just to get to one good one. I know when to trust it and when to ignore it. I know when to say, "Try again, but this time with a little more bite."

Writing used to be a lonely process for me. Now, it feels like a conversation. And that's made all the difference.

If you've ever felt blocked, if you've ever doubted your voice, if you've ever wanted to write something and didn't know how to begin, just know this: the words are already in you. AI just helps you find them faster. And you still get the final say. Always.

Prompts I Swear By

If you've ever typed something like "write me a blog post about creativity" into ChatGPT and ended up with a bland wall of text, you're not alone. Generic prompts get generic results. They're like asking a stranger at a party, "Tell me something interesting." You might get a polite answer, but probably not a great story. Once I realized that, everything changed.

The trick isn't writing perfect prompts. The trick is treating your prompt like a conversation starter. Something with tone, attitude, and just enough detail to give the AI direction without boxing it in. Let me show you how that plays out in real life.

When I'm trying to write a blog post, I never start with "write me a blog post." I start with something like, "Can you help me write an opening paragraph for a post about creative burnout that feels honest, a little raw, and sounds like I'm talking to a friend over coffee?" That extra context changes everything. The AI doesn't just spit out a formal intro. It gives me something warmer, more conversational, something I can actually use or tweak without cringing.

Sometimes I'll prompt it with a tone reference instead. I'll say, "Write this like a mix between a stand-up comic and a TED Talk speaker who just had their third coffee." That sounds ridiculous, but it works. The output is punchier. More surprising. More fun to read and rewrite.

When I'm stuck on a headline, I don't ask for "ten headlines." I ask for "ten bold, weird, slightly dramatic titles for a post about creative resistance—like something you'd click at midnight even if you were tired." I give it a scenario. I paint a mood. The better the setup, the better the response.

And when I'm writing something long, like a story or a guide, I build prompts step by step. I ask for an outline first. Then I pick a section and ask for a draft. Then I tell it, "This is a good start, but make it sharper and cut the filler." I use my own notes as part of the prompt. I paste in my half-written paragraph and ask it to continue in the same rhythm. It's not one and done. It's a loop.

Prompts that work well are the ones that sound like how you actually think. Don't try to sound technical or smart or formal. Just talk to the tool like it's a helpful creative partner who gets your vibe.

If you don't know where to start, begin with your audience. Who are you writing for? Say that in your prompt. Say, "Write this for someone who's creative but always second-guessing their work." Or, "Write this like I'm trying to convince my overthinking best friend to finally post her art online." The more specific the reader, the clearer the tone.

You can also drop in your own phrases. If you wrote one great sentence but don't know how to continue, paste it into the chat and ask, "Can you keep writing in this same voice, keeping the energy and pacing?" Or say, "This line sounds like me. Use it as a reference for the rest."

When I need a confidence boost, I even prompt the AI to hype me up. I'll write a sentence and ask, "Can you rewrite this like I've already done the thing and I'm proud of it?" It turns anxiety into momentum.

At the end of the day, your prompts don't need to be perfect. They just need to feel like you. Speak how you speak. Be honest about what you're trying to say. Treat the tool like it's there to help shape your thoughts, not replace them.

Once you find the rhythm, you'll realize writing doesn't have to be slow or painful. It can be fast, playful, weird, and deeply satisfying. You'll still have to edit. You'll still have to cut and refine. But you'll never have to face a blank page alone again.

And that's a writing habit worth building.

Fixing the Funk

Sometimes the writing looks fine, but something's off. The flow is clean. The grammar is solid. But when you read it back, it just doesn't hit. It sounds like it's trying too hard. Or not hard enough. It feels flat, overpolished, lifeless. That's the funk. The funk is what happens when the words make sense but don't make you feel anything.

You'll know it when you see it. That blog post you wrote with AI that reads like a brochure. The social caption that technically says the right thing but doesn't make you want to post it. The email that hits all the talking points but has no spark. It's functional, but forgettable.

Here's the good news. The funk is fixable. You don't need to throw everything out. You just need to bring the pulse back.

When I hit that kind of writing, I do one thing first. I stop editing and start asking questions. What am I really trying to say here? What do I wish this sounded like? Who am I picturing on the other side of this sentence? Those answers help me steer the tone. They bring the writing back to a place that feels connected instead of automated.

A lot of times, fixing the funk is about rewriting the intro. That's where the tone gets set. If your first paragraph sounds like it was written by an intern on autopilot, everything that follows will feel the same. Try starting with a story, a confession, or a weird metaphor. Something personal. Something risky. You can always clean it up later. But if the first few lines don't sound like a real person with something real to say, the rest won't carry weight.

Another fix is reading the writing out loud. It's one of the fastest ways to hear what's wrong. If a sentence makes you stumble or cringe or feel like you're reading off a teleprompter, cut it. Rewrite it in your speaking voice. Imagine you're explaining the idea to someone you know well. Say it how you'd actually say it.

Sometimes I'll even talk to the AI out loud, then transcribe that into the prompt. I'll say, "Okay, I'm trying to explain how using AI helped me launch a product, but I don't want it to sound like a sales pitch. I want it to sound honest, kind of funny, but still sharp." Then I type that into the chat and ask it to rewrite what I've got. That shift almost always improves the rhythm.

Another trick is to punch holes in your own draft. Take the AI's output and challenge it. If it uses vague language, ask, "What do you actually mean by that?" If it makes a bold claim, follow up with, "Can you prove it?" If it repeats the same phrase three times, change it. The funk lives in the lazy parts. The parts that didn't get questioned.

You can also fix tone by getting messier. If everything feels too neat, add a line that breaks the pattern. Drop in a question. Use a shorter sentence. Or a run-on one that spirals a little like this. Imperfection brings energy. And energy is what cuts through the noise.

The final fix? Give it space. If you've been staring at the same paragraph for an hour, walk away. Come back tomorrow and read it like someone else wrote it. You'll see what's missing. You'll know what to keep and what to cut.

Not every draft will shine on the first try. But AI gets you closer, faster. And once you know how to fix the funk, you'll never be stuck in it for long.

You don't need to sound perfect. You just need to sound like someone worth listening to. And that starts with being honest on the page—even if it's a little messy, a little awkward, and a little weird at first.

That's what makes it yours.

Try This Now

This challenge is simple. It's not about writing a masterpiece. It's about writing something quickly, revising it with clarity, and ending up with a piece of writing you'd actually share. It can be a post, a short story, a newsletter draft, or even a caption. What matters is that you go from blank page to finished piece without getting lost in the fog.

Start by choosing a topic you care about. Doesn't have to be deep. It can be light, weird, personal, funny, or just something you've been meaning to write about but keep putting off. What matters is that it's yours.

Once you have your topic, ask AI to help you get started. Don't just say, "Write this for me." Give it direction. Something like, "Help me write a short, casual piece about how I get back into flow when I feel creatively stuck. I want it to sound like I'm texting a friend, with a little humor and a little honesty."

Use whatever it gives you as a starting point. Don't copy it word for word unless it feels spot-on. Take the best parts and run with them. Add your own lines. Rewrite the awkward ones. Cut anything that sounds off or overly clean. You're aiming for tone over polish. Energy over structure.

Once you've got a rough draft, read it out loud. Ask yourself if it sounds like you. If it doesn't, pick one paragraph and rewrite it in your actual voice. Not your writing voice. Your speaking voice. Say it how you'd say it if you were on a call with someone you trust.

Then paste that paragraph into the AI and ask it to rewrite the rest of the piece in the same tone. This keeps the personality intact across the whole thing. You're shaping the draft like a sculptor, not stamping out a template.

Now do a second pass. Tighten the beginning. Drop in a better hook. Make sure there's one line that punches through with clarity or emotion. Something that makes the reader nod, laugh, or pause. That one moment is what ties the whole thing together.

When you're done, give it a title. Don't overthink it. Pick a line that fits the vibe, or ask AI to suggest five that match the tone. Choose the one that hits.

And that's it. You wrote something. You edited with intention. You used AI to move faster, but you didn't let it speak for you. You stayed in control. You made the final call.

Do this a few times a week and your writing will evolve quickly. You'll stop hesitating before you start. You'll know how to fix awkward drafts. You'll be able to generate ideas, write faster, and still sound like yourself. You'll become someone who writes with confidence, even if you still hate writing half the time.

This isn't about being a perfect writer, it's about being a consistent one. Someone who shows up, does the work, and lets the tool do what it does best—assist, not lead.

Try this now. Pick your topic. Write it fast. Shape it well. Share it if you want. Or save it as proof that yes, you really can write like you.

Chapter 13: AI Art Bootcamp

You don't have to be an artist to make art anymore. That sentence used to sound like an insult. Now, it's just the truth.

With the rise of AI image tools, anyone can create vivid, surreal, beautiful, or bizarre visuals using only words and curiosity. You don't need to draw. You don't need fancy software. You don't even need to know what you're doing at first. You just need to be willing to try, tweak, and explore. This chapter is your playground.

We're going to cover how to use free and easy tools to turn text into art. You'll learn how to write better prompts, how to refine results, and how to bring your ideas to life in ways that surprise even you. Whether you want to design a book cover, make social content, create mood boards, or just make weird stuff for fun, this chapter will show you how to make visuals that feel personal and expressive.

And just like with writing, this is about collaboration, not control. AI will give you something. Your job is to guide it, shape it, and decide when it's done. The tools can't read your mind, but they can read your vision—if you learn how to speak their language.

You don't need a background in design, you just need a little direction and the right kind of messy mindset. Art isn't about perfection. It's about feeling something.

Let's get weird, get visual, and turn your ideas into images.

RunwayML Rambles

The first time I opened RunwayML, I didn't know what I was doing. I had no design skills, no visual arts background, and no clue what half the buttons meant. I just had an idea in my head and the curiosity to see what would happen if I typed it out.

I wrote something like, "a floating city made of glass and vines, glowing under a purple sky." I hit generate.

A few seconds later, my screen filled with a wild, slightly eerie image that looked like a dream I didn't know I had. It wasn't perfect. Some parts were warped. The glass looked more like plastic in places. But it sparked something. I tweaked the prompt. I added details. I removed a few words. Each time, the image changed. Each time, I got closer to what I wanted, even though I hadn't known what that was at the start.

That's the magic of RunwayML. It's a visual playground disguised as a tool. You don't need to know how to draw. You don't need to understand layers or composition or any of the things traditional art programs expect. You just need an idea and a willingness to experiment.

RunwayML works best when you approach it like you're collaborating with a slightly surreal, very enthusiastic artist who doesn't sleep. You feed it phrases. It paints. You give it feedback. It adjusts. And the more you work with it, the more you start to understand what it responds to.

For example, adjectives matter more than you think. "A cat" will give you something basic. "A mischievous neon cat sitting on a rainy fire escape" gives you a vibe. And if you're trying to match a certain style, you can name it directly. Say "in the style of a watercolor illustration" or "like a scene from a Wes Anderson film." The tool won't always nail it, but it'll lean in that direction.

The first few images you make might not be great. That's part of the fun. They'll be strange, glitchy, and sometimes a little haunting in ways you didn't expect. But if you treat those early results like sketches instead of finished pieces, you'll start to see the potential inside them.

RunwayML also lets you upscale and enhance images when you find something you love. You can zoom in, fix the rough edges, or even blend two results together. But I usually wait until I've explored a few variations before doing any of that. It's easy to fall into the trap of polishing something that isn't quite there yet.

What surprised me most was how much the process felt like writing. You're using prompts, refining language, editing tone. But instead of paragraphs, you're shaping visuals. You're not just describing something—you're creating a version of it, one word at a time.

That overlap between language and image is where RunwayML really shines. It makes you think about your ideas differently. It forces you to slow down and consider what you're actually trying to express. Do you want a peaceful feeling or tension? Are you trying to evoke a place, a memory, a mood?

Sometimes I'll write a short paragraph about an idea first, then pull key phrases from that into RunwayML. That helps me stay connected to the story behind the image, even if the result is abstract. Other times, I'll use the visuals to inspire writing. I'll generate an image and then write a caption or a scene that fits the vibe. The process goes both ways. That's what makes it fun.

You don't need to be a visual thinker to use this tool. You just need to be open to what shows up.

And when something hits—when you see a piece of your imagination take shape right in front of you—it's hard not to want more.

That's how this tool gets into your creative bloodstream. Quietly. Weirdly. All at once.

Prompts That Pop

A lot of people think AI art is just about clicking a button and seeing what happens. And sure, that works for a while. But if you want to make images that feel intentional—images that tell a story or carry a specific mood—you've got to learn how to prompt with purpose.

Good prompts aren't just descriptions. They're directions. They tell the AI what to focus on, what to emphasize, what kind of world to build. A weak prompt gives you mush. A strong one gives you magic.

Let's start with what makes a prompt weak. If you type something like "a tree," the AI has nothing to go on. It might give you a pine tree or a cartoon tree or a realistic tree on a hill. There's no vibe. No story. No direction. You get a picture, but you don't get art.

Now take that same idea and shape it into something more alive. Try "a twisted willow tree on a foggy cliff, roots hanging off the edge, lit by a pale green moon." Suddenly, you've got mood. You've got color, setting, tension. You've got an image that *feels* like something. That's the difference.

The trick to writing better prompts is thinking like a director. Imagine the scene in your mind, then describe what you see, hear, and feel. Not just objects, but lighting, emotion, texture, even movement. AI tools respond to sensory detail. The more you include, the more they have to work with.

If you want a cyberpunk city, don't just say "cyberpunk city." Say "neon-lit alleyways under heavy rain, flickering signage in Japanese and English, smoke rising from sewer grates, reflections on the wet pavement." You're not just building a place—you're setting a tone.

It also helps to reference artistic styles or mediums. You can say "in the style of a vintage comic book" or "like a 1970s sci-fi paperback cover." These cues don't just shape the image—they give it character. Want something surreal? Add "dreamlike" or "melting" or "gravity-defying." Want something cute and minimal? Add "pastel" and "flat design" and "children's book style."

Don't be afraid to get weird with it. Some of the best images come from combinations that shouldn't make sense. A prompt like "a jellyfish shaped like a chandelier floating through a dusty cathedral" might sound strange, but it will give you something unforgettable. AI thrives on unexpected pairings.

Another tip: avoid overloading your prompt. If you cram in ten unrelated ideas, the AI will get confused and average everything out. Stick to one central image or concept per prompt.

You can always build more complexity by adding layers in future iterations.

When you find a prompt that hits, save it. Tweak it. Run it again with small changes. Keep a running list of what works for you. Over time, you'll start building your own visual language— the themes, textures, and tones that feel like *you*.

One thing that helps is writing the prompt before you open the art tool. That keeps you focused on the image you actually want, not just what the interface suggests. You're not here to react. You're here to create.

And when the image finally appears—when it looks almost like what you pictured—it's a rush. Not just because it looks cool, but because you know it came from your imagination, not just the algorithm.

That's the point of learning to prompt with intention. You're not just typing words. You're directing a scene. You're pulling something abstract out of your mind and turning it into something real.

And when you do it well, it shows.

Save It, Share It

Once you start generating images that feel right, that moment hits you. The screen lights up with something weird and beautiful, and your first thought is, okay, now what?

It's tempting to just keep making more. One good image leads to the next prompt, then another version, then another style. Before you know it, you've got a folder full of visuals and no plan. That's not a bad thing, but if you never stop to save or share your work, it stays trapped in a loop. A quiet gallery with no visitors.

The truth is, part of the creative process is knowing when to call something finished, even if it's not perfect. AI will always give you another version if you ask. But at some point, you have to decide that this one is the one. The lighting is off in a few spots. The colors might not match your mood perfectly. But it works. It hits. It says something. That's enough.

Saving your work means taking ownership of it. It means looking at the thing you made and saying, I want to keep this. Sometimes that's as simple as creating a folder for images you're proud of. Other times it's about curating a series that tells a story or exploring variations on a single concept. This isn't just file management. It's a way of building your creative archive.

And when you're ready, sharing takes it to the next level.

Sharing AI art can feel vulnerable, especially when you didn't paint every pixel or sketch every line by hand. But what you did do was dream it, direct it, shape it. You brought it into existence. That counts.

Start small if you need to. Share one image on your social feed with a caption about how it made you feel. Post it in a group chat with a "look what I made." Drop it into a community space where other creatives are experimenting with the same tools. You're not just showing off. You're inviting a conversation. You're saying, this is what I see. What do you see?

You'll be surprised how much connection can come from a single image. It doesn't have to go viral. It just has to resonate with someone. And when it does, you start to realize that this process isn't just about creation. It's about communication.

You're not just making things for yourself. You're offering up pieces of your imagination. And that kind of generosity—even in digital form—can shift something in you.

The more you share, the easier it gets. You learn which images feel most like you. You see what others respond to. You get better at trusting your own taste. And if you want to go further, you can start building collections. Use your images as album covers, story starters, digital prints, mood boards. Pair them with writing. Turn them into products. You get to decide what they become.

But it starts with saving the ones that matter. Claiming them. Giving them a home. And then, when the time feels right, letting them out into the world. Not because they're perfect.

But because they're yours.

Try This Now

You've played with prompts. You've seen images appear from nothing more than your words. You've felt that flicker of connection when one of them actually looks like the idea in your head. Now it's time to shape that energy into something you can hold onto. Not just another round of image generation, but a creative set with meaning behind it.

Pick a feeling to start with. Not a subject, not a style. A feeling. Something personal, something real. Maybe it's wonder. Maybe it's restlessness. Maybe it's nostalgia for a version of yourself that only exists in late-night memories. Whatever it is, name it. That's the heartbeat of what you're about to make.

Now open your favorite AI art tool. Keep that feeling in focus. Start describing what it looks like. What colors it wears. What kind of places it might live in. What would it look like if you gave it shape, texture, space. Let your words build a visual that expresses the emotion, not just the concept.

Generate three to five images from this place. Don't overthink the prompt. Let it shift as you go. You're not trying to get it right. You're trying to get it out. Each image doesn't need to be perfect on its own. Together, they'll form something bigger. A set. A mood. A kind of unspoken narrative.

Once you've got your images, line them up. Look at them as a group. Ask yourself what they're saying together that they couldn't say alone. Is there a common thread? A contrast that makes the others stand out more? Rearrange them if you need to. Trim the set down if something doesn't fit. Let your eye guide the flow.

Now write something. Not a caption. Not a summary. Just a few lines about where this set came from. What it felt like to make it. Why it mattered in that moment. Think of it as a note to your future self. The you who might stumble back across these images in a few months and wonder what they were about.

Save everything. Give the set a name, even if it feels silly. Especially if it feels silly. A name makes it real. Makes it yours. And if you feel brave, share it. Post the full set. Send it to a friend. Use it as the start of a story or a soundtrack or a product idea. Use it as a way back into yourself the next time you feel stuck.

This is how AI art becomes more than a tool. It becomes part of your creative rhythm. Your way of processing, expressing, imagining. Your way of speaking through images when words feel too small.

Try this now, start with a feeling, and see what it becomes.

Chapter 14: AI in My Daily Grind

Up until now, we've looked at how AI can help you make art, write stories, build products, and reflect on your purpose. But what about the rest of the day? The in-between hours, the mental clutter, the part where life feels less like a creative sprint and more like a slow uphill climb?

This chapter is about the quiet power of AI in the daily grind.

We're talking about the emails you keep avoiding. The to-do lists that grow faster than you can check things off. The calendar that won't stop shifting. The voice memos you never listen to, the notes you never organize, the projects that live in six different apps and none of them feel quite right. AI can help with that too.

Not in a flashy, life-changing way. But in small, sustainable ways that free up just enough energy for you to think clearly again. You'll learn how to use it as a second brain when yours is tired, a thought organizer when your mind is racing, a quiet helper that makes things just a little bit easier to manage.

This is not about becoming more productive for productivity's sake. It's about removing the friction that slows you down so you can spend more time doing what matters and less time wrestling with the mess.

You'll see how to turn AI into your habit buddy, your fast fix machine, your idea catcher. You'll build systems that don't feel like systems. And you'll come out with a better sense of how to let technology support your life without taking it over. Let's get into the details. This is where things get practical, personal, and surprisingly light.

Habit Buddy

Building habits is hard enough when you're motivated. It's almost impossible when your brain is tired and your day feels like a blur. You know what you want to do—wake up earlier, journal, move your body, write more—but somehow the momentum never sticks. You start strong, miss a day, miss another, and suddenly you're back at zero. This is where AI becomes more than a tool. It becomes your habit buddy.

Not a drill sergeant. Not a life coach. Just a patient presence that helps you keep track of what matters, without guilt-tripping you when things fall apart. It reminds you gently, supports you when you forget, and helps you reset without starting over.

I started using AI this way by accident. I was trying to build a morning routine that didn't overwhelm me. Nothing fancy. Just a short list of actions I wanted to do before checking my phone. Stretch, drink water, write a single sentence. That was it. But every time I tried to build a checklist or a calendar reminder, I ignored it. It felt like a task, not a rhythm.

So I opened ChatGPT and said, "Can you help me design a morning routine that feels light, flexible, and a little playful?" The response wasn't just a checklist. It had personality. It asked questions. It gave variations. And suddenly I had something I wanted to follow.

From there, I started checking in with it. I'd type things like, "I skipped journaling three days in a row. Help me start again without feeling behind." Or, "What's one tiny win I can aim for today that doesn't feel like a big deal?" And every time, the AI helped me reset without judgment.

That was the difference. It didn't scold me. It didn't push a streak. It just helped me return.

You can use AI to build your own version of this. Ask it to help you create a habit menu instead of a strict plan. Something that adapts with your energy. Ask it to check in with you at the end of the day. Ask it to keep track of how your habits shift week by week and reflect that back to you. You'll start seeing patterns. Not just in what you do, but in how you feel.

The more I used AI this way, the more consistent I became. Not because I was working harder. Because I was working with more awareness.

Some days, I ask the AI to help me stack my habits based on how much time I have. Ten minutes? Cool. Give me one habit that makes me feel clear. Thirty minutes? Let's build something a little deeper. It's like having a personal assistant who doesn't mind if I cancel and come back later.

The real gift here isn't just that AI remembers things. It's that it helps you remember who you're trying to be. Without shame. Without perfection. Just a little support in the right direction. That kind of consistency changes more than your calendar.

It changes how you feel about showing up for yourself.

Fast Fixes

Some days are smooth. Most are not. You spill coffee, miss a meeting, forget what you were supposed to do, and now your brain feels like static. This is the part of the day where creativity fades and stress takes the wheel. You're not looking for a breakthrough. You're just looking for something that works.

That's where AI can step in with what I call fast fixes.

A fast fix is not a life solution. It's not a productivity hack. It's a small way to get unstuck when everything feels like a mess. These are the moments when you don't want to think, you just want help. A quick sentence. A starting point. A calm voice that helps you sort your thoughts and get moving again.

I've used AI this way more times than I can count. I've opened a chat and said, "I have no idea what to write in this email. Help me start it." Or, "I need a gentle way to cancel a meeting without sounding flaky." Within seconds, I have a draft I can edit or copy or just use as a jumping-off point. That's the power of fast fixes. They skip the drama and get you to action.

One of the best things about AI is how fast it gives you options. You can describe what you're stuck on and it gives you five ways out. You can ask for tone help and it makes your writing sound calm when your brain is anything but. You can paste in a scrambled to-do list and ask it to organize your day based on urgency, not just order.

I've asked for meal ideas when I didn't want to think about food. I've asked for short pep talks when I felt scattered. I've asked it to rephrase messages when I was too frustrated to find the right words on my own. It's not about outsourcing your decisions. It's about clearing the fog so you can make better ones.

Sometimes, I'll even use AI to name what I'm feeling. I'll type out a messy paragraph like, "I can't focus, I feel behind, everything is loud and I keep switching tasks." Then I'll ask, "What's going on here, and how do I fix it in under ten minutes?"

It doesn't always nail it. But it helps. It gives me a lens. It reminds me I'm not broken, I'm just overwhelmed.

The key to using AI for fast fixes is honesty. Don't try to be impressive. Say exactly what's going on. If you're panicking over a deadline, say that. If you need to reschedule something because your brain is fried, say that. The more real you are, the more useful the response will be.

These little moments of clarity add up. They save energy. They reduce stress. They make it easier to move through the day without spiraling. Over time, you build a rhythm with it. You start knowing when to ask for help and when to trust yourself to push through.

You don't always need a big solution. Sometimes you just need a little help writing a sentence you can't figure out on your own. Sometimes you need your to-do list reordered so you can breathe again. Sometimes you need one idea for dinner that doesn't require a grocery trip.

That's the kind of help AI is good at giving. Fast. Focused. Zero judgment, and exactly what you need to keep going.

Voice Vibes

There's a difference between writing something and *sounding* like yourself when you write it. Most of us know how to hit send on a message that's clear enough. But how often do you stop and ask, "Does this sound like me?" Or better yet, "Does this sound like the version of me I want people to meet?" That's where voice comes in. And it's one of the most overlooked ways to use AI in daily life.

Your voice is not just your vocabulary. It's your rhythm, your tone, your pacing, your honesty. It's the energy people feel when they read your words or hear you speak. When it clicks, people remember what you said. When it doesn't, everything gets flattened.

I started playing with voice prompts out of frustration. I had to write a tricky message—something honest but delicate—and every draft I typed felt stiff or overly polished. So I asked AI to rewrite it like I was talking to a close friend. Just like that, the tone shifted. It didn't change the facts. It just sounded more like me. And it felt better.

Now, I use AI to adjust the vibe of anything I'm writing when I feel off. If I'm sending an email and I sound too formal, I'll ask it to soften the tone without losing clarity. If I'm writing a caption and I feel like it's too bland, I'll ask it to add energy or humor without trying too hard. If I'm drafting something public and it feels flat, I'll feed in a sentence I like and ask the AI to match the style for the rest.

It's not about faking authenticity. It's about helping your *actual* voice show up when you're too tired, too busy, or too in your own head to get it right on the first try.

You can also use AI to find your voice if you're not sure what it is. Paste in writing samples from times you felt confident, clear, or creatively alive. Ask the AI what it notices. What's consistent about your tone? What makes your writing stand out? Then ask it to help you shape new pieces using that style as a base.

This is especially helpful if you're writing across platforms and trying to stay consistent. You want your email newsletter to sound like your website, and your website to sound like your Instagram, and your Instagram to sound like your actual human self. AI can help you create templates that hold your tone, no matter what you're writing.

I've even used it for speech practice. I'll type, "I'm about to leave a voice message and I want to sound warm but direct. Can you help me phrase this in a way that feels kind without softening the message too much?" The results aren't always perfect, but they're enough to get me in the right mindset. And that changes everything.

When your voice feels aligned, your communication flows. You're not just transmitting information. You're connecting. You're creating tone. And in a noisy world, tone is what people remember.

Using AI to refine your voice doesn't mean outsourcing your personality. It means clearing the clutter so the best parts of you come through. The humor. The clarity. The calm. The confidence. The part of you that knows what you mean, even when the first draft comes out clunky.

Whether it's a text, a post, an email, or a pitch, your voice is the fingerprint on everything you send out, let it sound like you.

Even on your off days.

Try This Now

You don't need to overhaul your life to start using AI in your daily routine. You just need one moment, one stuck place, one little friction point where you can let the tool help—not because you're trying to be more productive, but because you want the day to feel lighter.

Start by thinking about your next hour. Not your next month. Not your next big project. Just the next slice of time. What's one thing you need to do that feels slightly annoying, awkward, or slow?

Maybe you have to send an email that's been sitting in your drafts. Maybe you need to write a description for something you're posting. Maybe your to-do list is a mess and you don't know where to start. Pick something small but real.

Now open a chat window and describe the problem like you're talking to a friend. Be honest. Say, "I've been putting off this message because I'm not sure how to phrase it without sounding too formal." Or, "I have five tasks and they all feel important, but I can't tell which one to start with." The more specific you are, the more helpful the response will be.

Ask for one version. Don't go down the rabbit hole of endless edits. Use what you get as a spark. Adjust it. Make it yours. Then send the message. Or reorder the tasks. Or post the caption. Take the action and move on. That's your win.

Then do it again tomorrow. Pick one moment in your day where you normally stall, and use AI to get unstuck. It could be a reminder, a suggestion, a draft, a rewrite. Whatever helps you move with less resistance. The goal is not to let AI take over. It's to let it carry a little of the load when your energy dips.

If you want to go deeper, keep a note on your phone with a few "everyday helpers" you've discovered. Short prompts that work for you. Like "Write this email like I'm being honest but not dramatic." Or "Help me make a list that doesn't feel like it's judging me." These shortcuts build your own toolkit. You start to move faster, and your day gets a little smoother.

And once in a while, take a minute to reflect. What did AI make easier this week? What did it let you skip or simplify or breathe through? This is where the quiet magic shows up. In the spaces where life feels less like a struggle and more like something you're shaping.

Try this now. you don't have to be brilliant. You just have to be a little more supported than you were yesterday.

Chapter 15: What's Next for My Creative Soul

By now, you've made a lot. You've written, built, designed, explored. You've tried tools, bent prompts, followed ideas through, and probably surprised yourself more than once. You've seen how AI can unlock your creativity, speed things up, and help you build without burning out.

So now what?

This chapter isn't about the next tool or trend. It's about the part that comes after the doing. The part where you sit with what you've made, think about what it means, and decide how you want to keep growing.

It's easy to get caught in the loop of creation. Generate. Post. Move on. But real creative growth comes from stepping back sometimes. Looking at the themes that keep showing up. The things that still scare you a little. The work that makes you feel most like yourself. Those are the things worth paying attention to.

This chapter is where we zoom out. Not in a distant, dreamy way, but in a grounded, personal way. You'll think about where you want to take your creative energy next. What you want to deepen. What you want to try that you've been avoiding. Who you want to connect with. What kind of work you want to be known for—not by the internet, but by yourself.

We're not chasing goals here, we're following creative instincts. We're tuning into what matters, now that the noise has cleared.This is the part where you make creativity feel like home.

Let's figure out where your soul wants to go next.

2025 Crystal Ball

Trying to predict the future used to feel like a guessing game. Now it feels like a survival skill. With AI evolving fast, creative tools changing monthly, and trends moving at the speed of a TikTok scroll, it's easy to wonder what your creative life will even look like a year from now. But the goal here isn't prediction. It's vision.

This is your moment to stop reacting and start imagining. Not in a vague way, but in a way that's personal and grounded. The point of the 2025 crystal ball isn't to map out your whole future. It's to give shape to a version of you that feels exciting, possible, and slightly out of reach in the best way.

Start by closing your eyes and imagining this: It's one year from now. You're in a space that feels like your version of creative flow. What are you working on? Who are you sharing it with? What kind of tools are part of your routine? What no longer feels like a struggle?

This isn't about a dream life that floats ten years away. This is one year out. A version of your creative self that could exist with the right mix of intention, courage, and momentum.

I like to use AI to help pull that vision into language. I'll open a chat and type something like, "Help me describe a version of myself one year from now if I stay consistent with my creative practice." The response is always interesting. Not because it's perfectly accurate, but because it reflects things I haven't said out loud yet.

I'll follow it up with more prompts. "What might I be creating in April of next year?" Or, "What kind of people would I be collaborating with if I kept showing up?" I tweak the answers until something clicks. It's not about pretending the future is locked in. It's about seeing what direction feels most alive.

Sometimes I'll write a letter from future me. Not a polished one. Just a stream-of-consciousness note about where I'm at, what I've built, what habits stuck, what surprises came. Then I ask the AI to clean it up just enough so I can read it back with clarity. It's strange and powerful to see yourself reflected in that way.

The future version of you doesn't need to be impressive. It just needs to feel true. Maybe you've finally launched a small digital shop. Maybe you're consistently writing and sharing your work. Maybe you've learned to rest without guilt, and that's what's opening creative doors. Whatever it is, write it down. Make it visual. Use images, colors, playlists. Whatever helps it feel less abstract.

The idea here is not to predict 2025. It's to meet the version of you who's already on the way there.

Once you've done that, ask yourself this: What would that version of me want from me today? Not what would they expect. What would they hope I'd try, risk, or let go of? That question becomes a compass.

Every time you get stuck, burned out, overwhelmed, or uninspired, you can return to that future version and say, "What now?" And the answer will usually be something simple. Make the thing. Rest for real. Say yes. Say no. Keep going. You're closer than you think.

You're not looking for certainty. You're building creative trust, that's the real power of your 2025 crystal ball.

It's not about where you're going, it's about who you're becoming on the way there.

Leveling Up

Leveling up sounds like doing more. Publishing faster. Getting louder. Expanding everything until your calendar breaks and your brain starts running on fumes. But real growth doesn't always look like that. Sometimes it looks like stripping things down. Focusing on fewer projects with more care. Saying no to things that don't match your values. Saying yes to ideas that scare you for the right reasons.

This part of the journey is about deciding what your next level actually is—not what the internet says it should be.

For some people, leveling up means going from hobby to income. For others, it means creating without hiding. It might mean starting a newsletter. Or finally charging for your work. Or creating just for yourself without needing permission or praise. It might even mean quitting something that's no longer yours to carry.

AI tools can make growth faster, but they can't define what growth means for you. That's your job. Your level up is yours alone. And it starts by asking better questions.

What am I ready to outgrow?

What do I want to go deeper into?

What would feel like a creative risk worth taking?

I ask myself these every few months. Not to overhaul everything, but to realign. To make sure I'm still choosing what matters, not just coasting on habits that got comfortable. Sometimes leveling up means learning new tools. Exploring new platforms. Asking the AI to show you things you haven't tried yet.

Other times, it means refining what you already do. Making your writing sharper. Your voice clearer. Your work more intentional.

Either way, the goal isn't scale. It's depth. One of the best things I ever did was pick a project and decide to go all in. Not to make it perfect. Just to make it real. I used AI to speed up the messy parts, but I stayed present through the heart of it. I stopped skimming my own work. I read it out loud. I pushed past my own patterns. The difference showed. People could feel it. And more importantly, so could I.

That's what happens when you level up with intention. You stop moving for the sake of motion. You start creating in a way that feels anchored, aligned, and sustainable.

The other piece of this is emotional. Growth is uncomfortable. Even good growth. You'll start sharing things that feel more personal. You'll start taking up more space. You'll hear your own voice more clearly, and that might scare you at first. That's normal. That means it matters.

AI can't help you feel less afraid. But it can help you move through fear faster. It can help you write the scary post. Pitch the idea. Draft the outline. Say the thing you were going to keep to yourself. It gives you momentum when your confidence lags. It reminds you that progress is always within reach—even when it feels far away.

If you're not sure what your next level is, look at your current creative life and ask yourself one simple thing: What would make this feel more like mine? More honest. More focused. More fun. More powerful. Choose one area and work on that. Let the rest follow.

You don't have to upgrade everything. You just have to upgrade your connection to the work.

That's how real growth happens.

Finding My People

Creating in a vacuum works for a while. You tinker, test, explore in peace. You learn how to use the tools, figure out your style, and maybe even build something you're proud of. But at some point, the creative process starts asking for something more. Not bigger, just more human. More connected. That's when the search begins—not for more content, but for your people.

The ones who get it. Who see what you're trying to do before it's polished. Who make you feel like you're not building alone. AI can help you move faster. But real momentum comes when someone else says, "Me too."

I didn't always think community mattered. I liked working solo. I liked figuring things out on my own. But when I started sharing small pieces of what I was working on—sketches, messy drafts, half-formed ideas—I was surprised by the responses. Not applause. Just connection. Curiosity. Conversations that made me better. That's what finding your people feels like. It's not networking. It's resonance.

You can use AI to start the process. Ask it to help you write a post that explains what you're working on and why. Use it to summarize your project in a way that's easy to share. Ask it where people like you hang out online. What kinds of communities, newsletters, or subcultures might feel like home. The tool can't build relationships for you, but it can make the first steps easier to take.

Start by showing up where people are already doing what you love. Join a small creative Discord. Comment on a Substack that feels like your vibe. Share a thought on a topic you've been circling. Don't worry about being the smartest or loudest person in the room. Focus on being honest. Being consistent. Being curious. The right people will find you when your voice is clear.

And if you want to create your own space, do it. Use AI to help you shape it. A tiny newsletter. A three-person accountability group. A community around a shared tool, prompt, or idea. You don't need hundreds of followers. You just need a few people who care enough to keep coming back.

Creative isolation is comfortable. But it's not where your best work lives. That work needs friction. Feedback. Support. People who can ask better questions than the ones you're asking yourself.

When you find those people, everything shifts. Not because they do the work for you. But because they remind you why you started.

You get braver. You try bigger things. You stop hiding behind half-finished drafts. You let your ideas breathe in public. And in return, you get mirrors. Not perfect ones, but good enough to help you see your growth.

This doesn't happen all at once. It builds. One post. One reply. One message. One creative win shared in a group chat that turns into a conversation that turns into a collaboration that turns into something real.

You won't find your people by chasing attention. You'll find them by showing up as yourself, again and again, even when it's awkward or unclear. Especially then, and when you do, the creative process becomes something bigger than output. It becomes a space of belonging.

Let yourself have that.

Try This Now

Take twenty minutes. Not for planning. Not for producing. Just for listening—to yourself.

This is a creative check-in with your future in mind. A way to take everything you've built so far and ask, where is this going? Not in a pressure-filled, figure-it-all-out way. Just with curiosity.

Start by asking AI to help you write a letter from your future self. One year ahead. You can say, "Help me write a letter from me in April 2026. I want it to sound reflective and hopeful, like I've spent the year creating from a place of clarity." Let it start the letter. Then you take over.

Fill in the details only you know. What did you build? What did you learn? What did you finally stop doing? Who did you meet, and what did they help you see about yourself? Don't focus on achievement. Focus on experience. Emotion. Growth.

Once the letter is written, ask AI to help you name three themes. Not goals. Not checkboxes. Themes. Ideas that can guide how you show up creatively going forward. Maybe it's consistency. Or visibility. Or more play. Maybe it's deeper connection, or braver expression. Whatever comes up, write those three words down and keep them somewhere visible.

Next, ask yourself this question, out loud or in writing: If I trusted my creative instincts completely, what would I do next?

Let the answer come slowly. It might be something you've been avoiding. It might be something tiny that wants more room. Whatever it is, say it without judgment. Now, give that idea a tiny next step. Not a full plan. Just one nudge. One email to send. One piece to finish. One thing to release into the world even if it's not perfect.

You can also ask AI to help. Type, "Based on this idea, what's one small action I could take this week to move it forward?" Choose the one that feels the most doable. Then do it.

When you're done, check in with how you feel. Not just what you did, but how you felt while doing it. That's your compass. Follow what feels grounded, not just what looks impressive.

This whole process is yours to repeat anytime. It works as a reset, a review, or a ritual. You don't need to wait for burnout or a milestone. You just need a window of space, a little self-honesty, and a willingness to ask yourself what matters now.

Your creative soul doesn't need a schedule. It needs room to breathe. It needs reflection. And sometimes it needs a quiet push to remind you how far you've come and how much further you're ready to go. Try this now, let future you speak.

Then listen closely.

Chapter 16: My AI Unleashed Survival Kit

You've made it to the end of the book, but this isn't really the end. This is the point where the tools become yours, the rhythms become habits, and the experiments keep going long after the last page.

By now, you've seen how AI can support your creativity without stealing your voice. You've learned how to brainstorm, write, design, reflect, and even reset your mindset with a little digital help. You've explored the messy parts, the surprising parts, and the moments when you thought, "Wait, did I actually just make that?"

This chapter is your creative reset kit. A stash of essentials you can reach for anytime you're stuck, overwhelmed, or just need to remember why you started. Think of it like a digital sketchbook mixed with a first-aid kit for your creative brain.

You'll find some of the most useful prompts, exercises, and check-ins from this book in one place. You'll also get a few new ones, things designed to keep your momentum going even on off days. None of it is about being perfect. It's about staying connected—to your ideas, your pace, your weirdness, and your why.

Creativity with AI isn't a linear journey. It loops, it swerves, it resets. This kit is here for all of it. Let's stock your shelf so you never feel stuck staring at the blank page alone.

The Best Bits

Before we wrap, let's take a second to name the stuff that worked. Not everything. Just the pieces that stuck. The bits you underlined in your head. The moments that made you pause and think, I could actually use that.

This is your cheat sheet. Your greatest hits. The things to remember when the spark dims or the noise gets loud.

You learned that creativity doesn't start with inspiration. It starts with momentum. You don't need to wait for a perfect idea. You just need a good enough prompt and the courage to start shaping what shows up. AI is a tool that gives you permission to move sooner, not better.

You saw that your voice still matters more than anything else. No matter how sharp the output, no matter how clean the copy, your tone, your rhythm, your weird brain is what makes the work feel human. That doesn't go away with automation. It just means you have to listen for it more carefully.

You figured out that prompts are powerful. Not because they're perfect, but because they guide the process. Good prompts aren't magic spells. They're conversations. The better you get at asking the right questions, the more helpful your tools become.

You found ways to write without fear, generate images without drawing skills, make music without instruments, and launch ideas without waiting for someone else's permission. That's real creative freedom, even if it still feels messy.

You saw that using AI is not about doing more. It's about doing with more clarity. More intention. More honesty. You learned how to filter, refine, reset. You started noticing when something felt like you and when it didn't—and that instinct is everything.

You probably realized by now that the process is less about the tools and more about how you show up to use them. How you think. How you edit. How you connect the dots.

You also gave yourself space to reflect. You let your future self talk. You slowed down to ask what mattered. You learned to pause without quitting. That's how long-term creativity stays sustainable.

And maybe, most important of all, you started to believe that you don't have to choose between technology and creativity. You get to have both. You get to explore without apology. You get to build a life where the tools support the vision—not replace it.

Keep these truths close. Write them somewhere. Save them where you can find them on the hard days. Because those days will come. And when they do, you'll need a reminder that you've already done the work. You already know what to do. Start small. Stay curious. Use the tool. Trust your gut. Follow the energy.

And keep going.

Prompt Stash

Some days you know exactly what to say. Other days, you just need a little nudge. A question. A spark. A way in. That's what this stash is for. These are prompts you can use anytime you're stuck, tired, curious, or ready to explore but don't know where to begin.

They're not magic words. They're starting points. Adjust the tone, swap in your topic, make them weird. They'll work better when you make them yours.

If you need a writing boost:

I'm trying to write about [insert topic], but I don't want it to sound generic. Help me start with a sentence that feels human and surprising.

Rewrite this paragraph like I'm explaining it to a friend who's smart but easily distracted.

Give me three headline options for a post about [insert theme], and make them bold without sounding clickbaity.

If you're making visual art:

Generate an image that feels like [insert emotion], using a style similar to [insert artist or medium]. Think less literal, more dreamlike.

Create a surreal scene based on this sentence: "[insert your own sentence or story fragment]."

I want to build a mood board with images that combine [concept one] and [concept two]. What are five prompts I can use to explore that?

If you're brainstorming:

I have a vague idea about [insert idea]. Can you ask me questions that might help turn it into something real?

Give me five unusual angles on this topic: [insert topic]. I'm trying to think beyond the obvious.

What would this idea look like if it was a product, a story, and a visual metaphor?

If you're feeling stuck:

I can't seem to start today. Give me a creative micro-task I can complete in under five minutes that will still feel meaningful.

I'm second-guessing everything I make. Can you remind me why small creative wins matter?

List five things I've probably done this week that count as progress, even if I didn't notice them.

If you want clarity:

Based on what I've shared, what do you think I'm trying to say? Help me say it in one clean, honest sentence.

How would I explain this idea if I believed in it fully?

Describe my current creative path like a character arc from a novel. Where am I in the story?

These prompts are flexible. You don't have to use them word for word. Think of them as a lens. A way to see your work from another angle. A way to talk to the tools like they're collaborators instead of content machines.

The more often you use prompts like these, the more they become a habit. A shorthand between you and the tool. A shared language that makes everything move a little smoother.

You don't need a huge library. Just a few reliable entry points. The ones that bring you back to the page, the canvas, the idea— especially when your energy is low and your doubt is high.

Keep this stash close. Add to it. Make your own. And when you're stuck, reach for it like a creative compass.

One good prompt is all it takes to unlock what's already waiting inside you.

Daily Dose

You don't need a complicated system to stay creative. You just need a rhythm. Something small. Something steady. A touchpoint that reminds you what it feels like to create without pressure.

This is your daily dose. It doesn't have to be dramatic. It doesn't even need to be productive. The goal isn't to finish something every day. The goal is to keep the channel open. To stay in motion. To remind your creative brain that it's safe to show up, even if all you've got is ten minutes and a leftover idea from last week.

The best daily routines are the ones that adjust to your energy. Some days are quiet. Some are chaotic. Your practice should flex with both. AI helps with that. It can meet you where you are, whether you want to sketch something wild or just write a single sentence that feels true.

Here's how I use AI to shape a daily dose when I need structure without pressure: In the morning, I open a chat and type, "Give me one reflective question to write about for five minutes." The response could be deep or light, serious or playful. Whatever it is, I answer it. No edits. No backspace. Just a short burst of thought.

Later in the day, I might ask, "Suggest one quick creative task I can do in under fifteen minutes using only free tools." It could be generating an image, remixing a headline, rewriting a line of copy, or exploring a weird prompt. The task doesn't matter as much as the act of doing something.

At night, I sometimes ask AI to help me wrap the day. I'll type, "Help me reflect on one creative win I had today, even if it was small." The tool helps me zoom in on something I might've skipped. It makes me pause. Celebrate. Let the work land.

You can build your own version of this. Morning check-in. Midday microtask. Evening reflection. Or just one of the three, depending on your mood. It's not about being consistent every single day. It's about returning often enough that creativity never starts to feel far away.

The key is to keep it light. Don't turn it into another job. Think of it as stretching. A way to stay flexible, curious, and open. A way to keep your ideas moving so they don't get stuck waiting for the perfect moment to show up.

And if you miss a day? No big deal. The point of a daily dose isn't streaks. It's access. You always have access. Even after a break. Even after a week of nothing. All it takes is one small spark to start again.

AI makes that easier. It gives you a way in, even when your brain feels blank. It catches your scattered thoughts and turns them into starting points. It doesn't ask for brilliance. It just asks you to show up.

That's enough. If you want to take it a step further, create a note where you log your daily doses. One line per day. No pressure to explain. Just keep a list of what you made, what you thought about, or what prompt you responded to. Over time, you'll see your own creative patterns emerge. You'll notice what excites you, what drags you, what themes come back again and again.

That's how you build a practice. Not through discipline. Through attention. Try it tomorrow. One moment. One prompt. One line.

That's your daily dose.

Your Launchpad

You've read a lot. You've made some things, or thought about making them. You've seen how AI can help you create faster, deeper, stranger, smarter. But now comes the part that matters most. Not the theory. Not the tools. The practice.

This is your launchpad. Not the kind where you blast off in a blaze of hype and pressure. The kind where you step forward with clarity. One project. One post. One paragraph at a time.

What you've built through this book isn't just a toolkit. It's a way of thinking. A way of seeing creativity as something that doesn't have to wait for permission. You don't have to wait for inspiration. You don't have to wait for expertise. You don't even have to wait to feel ready. You just have to start.

Your version of this launch will be unique. Maybe it's finally publishing that story idea you've been sitting on. Maybe it's building your first digital product. Maybe it's making art that's only meant to exist in your private archive. Maybe it's starting to talk about your process online, even if it feels raw.

Whatever it is, let it begin now. You can use AI to help map the path. Ask it to break down your idea into steps. Ask it to organize your chaos into something that feels doable. Use it to write your intro, your outline, your draft. Use it to clarify your audience or name your style or design your next move. Let it support you, but let your gut lead.

And if you feel like you've already forgotten most of what you read, that's okay. The best parts are already in motion. They're in your curiosity. In the questions you'll ask tomorrow. In the way you'll approach your next blank page with just a little less dread and a little more rhythm.

You can come back to this book anytime. But you don't need to wait until you feel stuck. Come back when you're ready to go further. Come back when your voice starts to shift and you want to shift your tools with it. Come back when you're ready to teach someone else what you've learned. You don't need to be a tech genius to thrive in this space. You just need to stay human in how you use it. Lead with ideas. Lead with play. Let AI be the shortcut, not the script.

This work is not about output. It's about connection. To yourself. To others. To the ideas that only you can bring into focus. So this is not goodbye. This is a beginning. One you can repeat, remix, and return to as many times as you need. Your creative brain is not a machine. It's not a brand. It's a wild, beautiful system of instincts, dreams, tangents, and sparks.

And now, it's got tools to match.

Go build something weird. Something small. Something loud or quiet or personal or public. Build something that makes you feel alive.

You're ready.

www.ingramcontent.com/pod-product-compliance
Lightning Source LLC
LaVergne TN
LVHW051321050326
832903LV00031B/3298